Madonna King is one of Australia's most accomplished journalists, having won awards for her *ABC Mornings* current affairs program. She writes across Fairfax, *Crikey* and *The New Daily*, and is the author of ten books, including the bestselling *Being 14* (ABIA shortlisted for non-fiction book of the year), *Fathers and Daughters*, *Ten-ager* and *L Platers*. She is also the biographer of 2006 Australian of the Year Professor Ian Frazer and former federal treasurer Joe Hockey. In 2018, Madonna served as chair of the Queensland Government's Anti-Cyberbullying Taskforce, set up in the wake of COAG. A fellow of the prestigious World Press Institute, she has served as a visiting fellow at the Queensland University of Technology and on the Walkley Advisory Board. Her website, www.madonnaking.com.au, provides further detail. She lives in Brisbane with her husband and two teenage daughters.

🐦 @madonnamking

Think Smart Run Hard: Lessons in Business Leadership from Maxine Horne

Hockey: Not Your Average Joe

Ian Frazer: The Man Who Saved a Million Lives

A Generous Helping: Treasured Recipes from the People of Queensland (with Alison Alexander)

Bali 9: The Untold Story (with Cindy Wockner)

Catalyst: The Power of the Media and the Public to Make Change

Being 14: Helping Fierce Teens Become Awesome Women

Fathers and Daughters: Helping Girls and Their Dads Build Unbreakable Bonds

Ten-ager: What Your Daughter Needs You to Know About the Transition from Child to Teen

L Platers: How to Support Your Teen Daughter on the Road to Adulthood

The inside story of Taskforce Argos, Detective Inspector Jon Rouse
and their mission to protect our children online

SAVING OUR KIDS

MADONNA KING

hachette
AUSTRALIA

hachette
AUSTRALIA

Published in Australia and New Zealand in 2023
by Hachette Australia
(an imprint of Hachette Australia Pty Limited)
Gadigal Country, Level 17, 207 Kent Street, Sydney, NSW 2000
www.hachette.com.au

Hachette Australia acknowledges and pays our respects to the past, present and
future Traditional Owners and Custodians of Country throughout Australia
and recognises the continuation of cultural, spiritual and educational practices
of Aboriginal and Torres Strait Islander peoples. Our head office is located on
the lands of the Gadigal people of the Eora Nation.

A catalogue record for this
work is available from the
NATIONAL
LIBRARY
OF AUSTRALIA
National Library of Australia

ISBN: 978 0 7336 5070 3 (paperback)

Cover design by Christabella Designs
Cover images courtesy of Shutterstock
Author photograph courtesy of Tyler Alberti
Typeset in Sabon by Kirby Jones
Printed and bound in Great Britain by Clays Ltd, Elcograf S.p.A.

MIX
Paper from
responsible sources
FSC
www.fsc.org   FSC® C001695

The paper this book is printed on is certified against the
Forest Stewardship Council® Standards. McPherson's Printing
Group holds FSC® chain of custody certification SA-COC-005379.
FSC® promotes environmentally responsible, socially beneficial
and economically viable management of the world's forests.

To Jon Rouse and the small army of global crime fighters who go into battle each day for our children. Their goal is to save those little ones being preyed upon by online sex predators. As parents, we need to understand their fight, and help them.

Contents

Author's note

The names of victims, except those already strongly in public use, have been altered in this text. So have the names (including online pseudonyms) of many of the abusers, who continue to glory in their notoriety. Some of the precise circumstances and operational names have also been altered in consultation with investigators, all with the intention of not giving away policing techniques or compromising future legal action. This has been done with the aim of creating a truthful and informative account of how investigators are hunting down evil and saving our children.

Part 1

Online and unsafe

1

The danger at home

'Bridget. Bridget. Dinner is ready.'

Bridget's mother raises her voice above the din around the family dinner table. Her fifteen-year-old is locked in her bedroom, ignoring the plea to join the rest of the family. But what Bridget's mother doesn't know is that, on the other side of that bedroom door, her smart, kind and sassy daughter is naked, tears trickling down her cheeks as she performs sex acts on herself, in full view of her laptop camera. Her tormentor is online. He is issuing directions. 'Do this.' 'Do that.' 'You don't want your parents to know about this, or the whole world, do you?' She knows this because he told her last night, and the night before, that if she doesn't acquiesce, use her school ruler in this way and her hand in that way, what she's now doing will be plastered all over the web.

This is the latest manifestation of a crime as old as crime itself: the exploitation of the vulnerable for money or sexual gratification. In the 2020s, more and more crime is happening in cyberspace, and the vulnerable are the internet's most prolific and most naive users, young people who find themselves caught in an evil web of networked manipulators. It's a world well known to Detective Inspector Jon Rouse APM, who for three decades has been a central figure in combating child sexual exploitation in all its forms, only to find that the victims are now innocently engaging predators who are enticing them to create pictures and videos that haunt them into submission.

Jon Rouse is also the central figure in this book. It was written with his cooperation, and the support of a global network of crime fighters, to highlight the dangers lurking on every computer screen and smartphone, and in every computer game, as well as the work done by those who never sleep to save victims like Bridget, who is late for dinner while living in a world of pain that is stealing her teen years and her innocence, and shattering those around her.

This crime of sextortion, a combination of the words 'sex' and 'extortion', where a victim is blackmailed to pay their attacker in one of two ways – with more-detailed sexual content or with money – has reached epidemic proportions, fuelled by both serious sex offenders and organised scammers targeting the most vulnerable. Up to 70 per cent of all new online sexual content police investigators are seeing is victim-produced, and much of it follows the same script. A child produces content for an adult who has tricked them into thinking they are a celebrity or influencer or someone just like them. The adult abuser then 'sextorts' or bribes the child for more lewd content, or money delivered as gift cards, cryptocurrency, vouchers or online gaming credits.

In Australia, according to eSafety Commissioner Julie Inman Grant, 75 per cent of those cases where the abuser is after more sexual content will involve tween and teen female victims. In those cases where offenders are chasing money – financial sextortion – teen boys are overwhelmingly being targeted. While most male victims are between fifteen and twenty-four years old, some are as young as ten. In at least one case, a teen has handed over $10 000 to his tormentors. Across both forms of sextortion, the victims are often vulnerable boys and girls, looking for connection. Many are bright sparks, lured into sending an initial picture – of their breasts or penis, for example – at the request of an attractive new online friend who they accepted as a connection. And then, SNAP! Often in just a few minutes, they are held hostage by their online captor, who admits to having made up a persona and who then starts to bark orders – or the images they have captured will be sent to the young person's parents, friends or classmates, or the world, to see.

Teen victims feel trapped, unable to tell their parents about their initial bad decisions to trust a person masquerading as someone else and to provide that first image. They find themselves doing more and more on the orders of their tormentor. They make more videos, or they get the money demanded – and their persecutors then demand even more because they know their victim can get it. The victims are everywhere: in small, remote outposts and big cities in Australia, and all over the rest of the world. In many cases, when investigators find the online content, they cannot find the victim; they are not sure where he or she might live. Australia receives many of its tips about online sex abuse from the Virginia-based National Center for Missing & Exploited Children (NCMEC). That's because US laws oblige tech providers to report suspicious online child abuse activities, including sextortion, to the centre. NCMEC says that in 2022 it received thirty-two million suspicious reports and passed them on to 150 countries. More than 180 000 were in some way related to Australia, with 32 000 finding their way to Australian authorities – a mix of information and actionable reports.

Michelle DeLaune is NCMEC's president and CEO. She provides this real-life example to highlight the speed with which teens, especially boys, are being trapped. Let's call this teen boy Tom.

8.07 p.m. – offender makes initial contact with Tom, who is a teenager.

10.07 p.m. – Tom shares sexually explicit imagery.

10.23 p.m. – offender sends blackmail message, threatening he will release imagery unless Tom pays money.

Two hours later, Tom 'expresses suicidal ideation and stops messaging'. A few hours later, the offender contacts Tom's girlfriend, shares the images and asks if she knows him. She responds that it is her boyfriend and asks when the picture was taken. The offender says he will ruin her boyfriend's life with the picture.

12.03 p.m. – only sixteen hours after the initial contact, the girlfriend responds that her boyfriend, Tom, has killed himself.

DeLaune says the bribery attempts quickly follow a teen's decision to provide an image. 'And it's very aggressive,' she says. 'It can happen in a matter of minutes, from the moment that a photograph is sent until the blackmail.' And that is driving panic amongst teens.

Financial sextortion (as opposed to sextortion demanding more explicit sexual content) as part of international organised crime syndicates is discussed later in this book, but for now, suffice to say its growth should have every parent and educator worried. In the United States in 2021, NCMEC received 139 reports of financial sextortion. The following year it received 10 000. In Australia, it's the same. Almost 4200 sextortion complaints were lodged in the 2021–22 financial year, up 55 per cent on the previous year. Inman Grant says it keeps her awake at night. 'It's an epidemic,' she says. The Australian Federal Police (AFP) has seen a hundred-fold increase in reports. 'It is a critical shift in our offender base,' says AFP Assistant Commissioner (Southern Command) Hilda Sirec.

Outside the bedroom doors of so many teens like Bridget and Tom, parents are lost. Why has their happy, gregarious teen become so withdrawn? Why are they refusing to attend school? Why aren't they eating? Educators, too, are finding more and more of the school day being taken up with what they see as a new, industrial-scale crime targeting tweens and teens. A multitude of platforms, including Facebook, Skype, Kik, Tinychat, Omegle, Wattpad and Snapchat, are being used. And what worries Susan McLean, a former police officer of twenty-seven years, is that the reported figures are just a microscopic indicator of how big the problem is. She believes less than one-quarter of targeted minors alert authorities, an estimate that is widely supported. 'The risk is enormous,' she says. 'It's not a matter of if, it's when your children will be contacted by a paedophile online.' McLean, who now educates parents, teachers and students about cyber safety, says every image will come from a bedroom or a bathroom: 'And they are the two places that digital devices and cameras should never ever be allowed. I see what happens and none of these kids, who are being extorted, are anywhere other than there.'

Detective Inspector Jon Rouse, who at the time of writing is nearing retirement after three decades of globally recognised and awarded work, and his small Queensland-based team, Taskforce Argos, have been involved in investigations and arrests across four continents. Rouse just shakes his head at the rise of sextortion, a new focus of his work: 'If you've seen what I've seen, you would not allow your child to take their phone into their bedroom.'

Rouse is Australia's elite online child sex abuse investigator, having drawn others from around the world to join efforts to shut down crime networks hidden deep inside the web – you'll meet many of these other crime fighters as you read on. He has seen the worst of the worst of human depravity. Children being raped on demand online. Small children being sexually abused, then holding up a piece of paper on which is written the name of the offender – the trophy he has requested. Rouse and his team of investigators have seen too many men with titles and big offices torture tiny figures and then distribute the images for like-minded predators to pore over. At first, as online capabilities cranked up, these were grainy images passed around via virtual bulletin boards or primitive messaging platforms. Now they can be full-blown movies, taken from every imaginable angle. Rouse has hugged mothers whose children have taken their own lives after being tormented and tricked online. He's travelled to every nook and cranny of the globe to bring abusers to justice. But you can see in his eyes the knowledge that investigators like him will only ever make a small dent in a crime that we don't talk enough about. His are sad eyes. And yet they are hopeful eyes, too, because every sickening image he sees, every movie that investigators find racing through cyberspace, offers hope that the small, anonymous figure screaming in pain or lying silent, as though they've stepped outside of themselves, will be plucked to safety before the next attack – hope that the child being sextorted tonight in her bedroom in Perth or Penrith or Paris will find the courage to tell an adult, who will report it.

To investigators in this online field, images are crime scenes, and they work night and day with others in the Federal Bureau of Investigation (FBI) and Interpol and law enforcement units in dozens of countries to wrap virtual crime scene tape around them and track down every clue. No borders exist in this crime. Victims can be in the same home as their perpetrators or on the other side of the planet from them. No-one can confidently estimate the number of children saved over the past twenty years or so, but everyone who does this work knows it runs into thousands and thousands: children rescued who have been groomed for years to be the sex toy for someone on camera, others liberated before the attacker strikes. Interview these officers and they speak of hope in the heartache, of finding and freeing children. Some talk about later attending a victim's university graduation, or hearing that they'd walked down the aisle, deliriously happy; their grins are broad when they tell those stories. But most don't want to meet the victims they've saved, because they know that one day, as the abused grow through their teens and into adulthood, they'll wonder how many people saw them being raped, witnessed the knife being held at their throat. Three-quarters of the eighty-five million images reported to NCMEC in 2021 was content previously seen, which means it was redistributed online by offenders over and over again. Michelle DeLaune says images and videos of sexual abuse can be circulated hundreds of thousands of times online for years after the abuse has ended – some will have been taken this year, others up to three decades ago.

The focus of the people like Jon Rouse who you will read about in the following chapters is saving children. 'My KPI isn't arresting the abusers,' Rouse says. 'It's rescuing the children.'

•

Sextortion is now the number-one issue for online child sex crime fighters, and it is close to rivalling online bullying in schools. Indeed, it is now becoming so common that it's splitting investigative resources dedicated to other serious online child sex abuse. Up to a million 'users' or members are believed to have joined clubs hidden deep inside the World Wide Web to trade and chat about child sex abuse; some of those clubs are detailed in the stories that follow. Most are sophisticated and multilayered, with full company-like structures, enormous security, and involvement in crimes ranging from rape on demand to the granting of bonus points to those members who can upload the sickening images and videos that become the most popular.

So how is someone like Bridget or Tom drawn in to the point where they will remove their clothes and take orders from a stranger who might be in Africa or Europe or America? The answer is *grooming*. This is the first step in a child being extorted and it simply means that the paedophile or scammer makes contact with a child and befriends them. Let's take the case of a teen girl, because this script is playing out, repeatedly, across Australia today. Rouse says at first, the perpetrator 'might spam 100 kids in the hope that maybe five or ten or even one or two will engage with them'. They'll choose those with accessible friends' lists on any of a dozen or so social media platforms, so they can claim to know others their target knows, and they will try to befriend several of them in case they need to point to mutual 'friends' as part of their fake story. Most times this is not a difficult task for the perpetrator. A big proportion of tweens and teens have publicly accessible friendship lists, and it is uncommon – in many of their circles, it's almost improper – to turn down a friend request from someone who says they know someone who knows someone else. In the case of a teen boy, the photograph of an attractive girl might pop up in the same way, and after a vague 'Hi, we know a few of the same people', they click as online friends. Then, with a connection made, they start talking online. This is the grooming process, before the new 'connection' moves to the next step: sending photographs. Often, the groomer will talk about popular bands and use language that mirrors that of their prey. They'll find common interests and build trust, based on a fake persona and bold lies.

In real life, the new connection is not Gracie, a fifteen-year-old from Melbourne, or Bill, who goes to a private school in the same city. It might be a 52-year-old male in the United States with a family in the next room, a convicted paedophile in Europe looking for a new target, or a 45-year-old teacher in Asia with a decade-long criminal secret. What is consistent, though, is that it will be a fake profile, and almost always, in the online space, the offender will be male – irrespective of whether their targets are teen boys or girls.

The talk will be teen talk. Often, it will touch on body parts and the idea of having sex. It's natural to be curious, especially when tween girls believe they are talking to another tween girl about what sex might be like, or how her breasts are oddly shaped. Boys, often excited that a girl – who is really an adult male predator – has shown interest in him and wants to show him her breasts, will consider reciprocating.

Perpetrator: Have u ever had sex?

Girl: I soo so so wish I could have sex it sound so jucy but weird

Perpetrator: Yes I have many times just do it when u r ready ok U can have with the rite guy u need someone that will be gentle and go really slow i know the perfect guy same one that taught me heheh give me your mobile, I'll get my friend to call you then you can discuss with him

It continues:

> *Perpetrator: Can I call u?*
>
> *Girl: No*

With the conversation ongoing and the 'grooming' complete, the fake profile then moves to stage two: convincing his prey to send a naked photograph or even a video. Often, he will suggest they talk somewhere else, on another platform – one that, as it happens, also allows videos to be passed back and forth, and where images can be freely swapped. As they chat, the online predator masquerading as a peer might send a photo of a young girl's breasts, claiming they belong to him; or a photo of a penis – it all depends on who he is targeting. Once his prey has been groomed and holds no suspicions about their new online friend, he'll ask: 'Why don't you send me something. We'll be even then, and no-one will ever know.' The next move is what makes our tweens and teens a hostage to lone predators and organised crime networks. A boy might send what is widely known as a 'dick pic', believing it is being received by the cute girl he is now considering meeting up with; his school formal is next year, so perhaps he could ask her to that, too. The thought that organised criminals are going to extort money from him will not cross his mind. Similarly, a girl might think she's chatting with a new peer friend. How refreshing to be able to talk to someone about this stuff, she thinks. 'See, mine are smaller than yours,' she might caption a photo, sent from the privacy of her own bedroom.

Perpetrator: Want to swap pics?

Girl: Wat pics?

Perpetrator: Naughty ones

Girl: Wat do you mean swap pictures?

Perpetrator: Ill send u one u take the same and send it back

Girl: And wat naughty is?

Perpetrator: No clothes and stuff

Girl: Y?

Perpetrator: I want to see more of u

Girl: What do u mean more?

Perpetrator: Like your body

Eventually she sends photographs of her breasts. As the chat goes on, she might even provide more intimate content. And this is the point where the disguised predator catches his prey. He might keep the ruse going for a bit longer, to get a close-up, or more detail, or a movie. 'I want to see more of you,' he might say, or 'I like your body.' But he doesn't really need anything else. He has a photograph and/or video of a young Australian tween or teen, male or female. And that will be the basis of his blackmail. In some instances, offenders doctor images to make the victim appear to be in an even more compromising position.

Rouse proves to me what is happening each night to many Australian teens. He follows the profile of an attractive US female golfer. It's a public page, with lists and lists of friends. Within thirty minutes, ten people want to become friends with Rouse. All of them want to link up in other ways, too, on other platforms where they can talk more privately. And every single one of those profiles, on investigation, is fake. 'They followed me only because I followed a page,' says Rouse. 'Now, you get some thirteen- or fourteen-year-old boys following that page, because she's an attractive sportsperson. And immediately, they'll be hit up by other young, attractive women. And then they'll be drawn into this conversation, and end up sending a dick pic.' What's the first thing Rouse advises? 'On your profile, make your friends list inaccessible. This is just their methodology 101.'

Many investigators believe the latest wave of self-generated content has part of its origins in the 'selfie', which first became a concern a decade ago. Since then, the evolution and power of 'influencers' have seen children – and some of their parents – going to enormous lengths to be noticed, which means accessible public profiles, where followers represent success and possibly even future fame. 'Don't people remember the Amanda Todd case?' Rouse says, more as a statement than a question. 'We are now seeing suicides in Australia and globally on this issue.'

•

Amanda Todd, a Canadian student, took her own life in 2012, at fifteen, after being blackmailed to expose her breasts. Her tormentor was sentenced to thirteen years' jail in 2022. Before Amanda's death, she posted a heartbreaking video online about the torment she'd suffered. Her mother, Carol, says it has now been viewed fifty million times. 'I don't even know if sextortion was a word when it happened to Amanda,' she says. Carol, who teaches digital literacy, says we need to confront the issue by first understanding that our own children are not exempt from being caught in a predator's net. 'Nobody wants to talk about words that have sex in them,' she says.

Carly Ryan, a South Australian fifteen-year-old, was the first person murdered in Australia by a man with a fake profile. He groomed her before developing an online relationship with her. Carly's mother, Sonya Ryan, says she's watched criminals evolve, along with the technology available to them, since her daughter was killed in 2007. 'But what hasn't changed is the vulnerability of youth,' she adds. 'The need for validation. The need for connection.' Sonya says no online safety education existed when Carly was murdered, and social media platforms have 'a lot to answer for in relation to keeping their users safe. Their focus seems to be profit and privacy at the expense of extremely young, vulnerable people.' Sonya says she had never heard of grooming before Carly was ensnared by a serial paedophile who called himself Brandon Kane. Both Carly and Sonya believed he was an eighteen-year-old musician from Melbourne. He wasn't. He was a fifty-year-old predator who would turn to murder. Sonya says she learned that Carly had been groomed over a period of eighteen months – now, according to DeLaune and Inman Grant, it can take a matter of minutes. 'We had no comprehension that criminals had migrated from offline to online,' says Sonya, 'so stranger danger had essentially migrated. Then, the idea that someone would use the internet to create a fake identity in order to groom a child – that was nowhere. It was a shock to the entire nation. I was completely clueless.'

The Carly Ryan Foundation, set up by Sonya, has put enormous effort into educating children and parents, as have other organisations, but most parents still don't believe it could happen to their child. AFP research shows 52 per cent of parents and other carers are not having conversations around this topic, unaware that it is a concern. Unfortunately, as Susan McLean points out, children want to be liked, and sex predators know what to say. The weekend before our interview, she counselled one disbelieving mother whose fifteen-year-old son was being sextorted. The mother told McLean, 'He's sensible. He's smart. He's a straight-A student.' McLean says, 'But good kids make bad choices.' She knows two teen boys who handed over $3000 to their persecutor. They were given a choice: pay up or post ten more naked photos within the next twelve hours. 'Even if they get $50 ... it's a good day's work for these creeps,' says McLean.

Many Australian schools are dealing with the fallout of these cases. One Sydney principal says she dealt with three big cases in 2022. She was relieved the students raised the alarm so the police could be alerted. 'But they were scared of their parents finding out,' she says. 'We had to be the ones who broke it to their parents.' She says the parents were shocked, believing it was almost impossible for their child to have been exploited in such a way. 'I've seen this happen to young people who are bright and intelligent, articulate, and they get sucked in,' the principal says. 'And I guess I stand there thinking, How did they get sucked into this? Because I wouldn't have expected that. So it must be even harder for their parents to understand.'

Investigators are now also seeing videos of six- and seven-year-olds – self-generated – pop up in the collections of child sex offenders arrested around the globe. Some of those are Australian children who set up a device on the floor and perform like an exotic dancer. Some parents encourage this behaviour, building their children's social media profile and following it, in the hope it provides fame and possibly fortune down the track. But going forward, this presents an almighty challenge. Do investigators shift their focus to this self-generated content that is finding its way into the wrong hands, and which will almost definitely be traded, with lives potentially being destroyed when that's revealed much later? Or do they focus on the man who might be in Mexico or the United States or the Philippines who is swapping rape videos of an unidentified two-year-old on the dark web? Or do they prioritise putting a dent in the burgeoning sextortion market to stem teen suicides, or addressing the likelihood of victims finding out the sex acts they were ordered to perform are still circulating on the web a decade later, when they have their own children?

And don't be fooled into thinking that the viewing of children being violated is a lesser offence than the 'contact crime' of violating them, and may warrant less attention. As we will later learn, there is an alarmingly high correlation between those caught and convicted of the possession of child sexual abuse videos or photos, and those who have assaulted a child. One crime feeds the other, whether it's the result of a recorded and shared assault, or the coercion of a teenager conditioned to share images of themselves at every opportunity.

'We have a very thin blue line that does this work,' says Jon Rouse. And it is they who have to make a difficult decision. Do they chase down and try and rescue an abused infant? Or educate parents about the ignorance of posting scantily clad photographs of their children on open websites or their own child's Insta account?

Or, says Rouse, do they try to put a stop to a teen producing their own graphic content on the orders of a predator while their parents are having dinner in the next room? Rouse won't show me all of the hour-long video he is talking about, just parts of it. Afterwards, I feel glad he made that decision. It starts with a teen girl, crying. She's in her bedroom. And she knows, before her tormentor orders her, what she will be asked to do. I wonder if she can hear her siblings or her parents nearby. She's forced to insert objects into her vagina, to play with herself, and to perform a list of sordid acts that goes on and on and on. At the end, before her abuser turns off the camera, he bids her farewell. She knows she will have to do this all over again, the following night, because if she doesn't, that video will be plastered all over the web for everyone to see.

'And that's a fairly typical case,' Rouse says. Investigators haven't found her yet. Another teen girl whose future is being stolen by a sextorter, just like Bridget and Tom.

2

From the dark room
to the dark web

It was Y2K, not online sex abuse, that saturated the work schedules of many people as 1999 crept closer to 2000. Y2K was shorthand for the year 2000, but it also referred to a computer programming shortcut that panicked the nation. Many programs only allowed two-digit years, not four – 99 denoted 1999. But what would happen when the millennium turned and 99 became 00? In finance circles and media newsrooms, prison systems and the public service, in small businesses and big corporations, an enormous amount of time, money and effort went into safeguarding IT systems. And that saw senior Telstra computer technician Geoffrey Robert Dobbs seconded from his home city of Brisbane to do some work in Melbourne.

Dobbs's file would later be stamped 'never to be released', and his case would serve as the impetus for changing every skerrick of policing directed at finding serious child sex offenders like him. Dobbs, a Queensland father, would be at the epicentre of political and policy discussions, too – about the dangers lurking in our suburbs, the use of technology to distribute abuse, the sheer volume of abuse that could be committed by a single offender, the modus operandi or grooming used to build the requisite trust to assault a child, and how long a paedophile could carry on with their crimes before being caught.

The case served as a salient reminder to parents that their children should not automatically trust the adult in whose care they were placed. Children needed to be taught that, sometimes, those they trusted most would turn out to be monsters, as happened with the dozens and dozens of children who Dobbs abused. If the case presented a silver lining, it was in the form of new ways in which the police decided to work, from the greater use of undercover operatives to a call for new laws that would acknowledge the horror and heartache delivered by child abuse. It also proved a weathervane for what was to come: a digital world in which cameras would become smaller and much more numerous, and the images they captured more easily stored and shared – and just as easily obscured.

While Dobbs was in Melbourne, a cassette jammed in his video camera, prompting him to have it fixed. A repairman subsequently found images of Dobbs sexually abusing children, and contacted police. Dobbs was arrested and charged in late 1999 with dozens of offences that had occurred during the short time he was in Melbourne. Indeed, a police search found 177 videotapes at his Melbourne home. The magnitude of this shocked seasoned officers, who would later identify a total of 122 victims in Victoria and Queensland. But what still plagues those who worked on this case is that, two decades later, more than fifty of those victims remain unknown. That's because Dobbs either could not remember who they were or refused to identify them. He signalled the scale of his depravity early on, revealing to Victorian officers that dozens of his victims were to be found in his home state.

Taskforce Argos, the Queensland-based unit charged with tracking down those sex offenders who use technology to ply their dark work, travelled to Melbourne and seized all the exhibits that were not required by Victorian court authorities. Everyone was hopeful Dobbs would spend a long, long time in jail. But he received a surprisingly short sentence over the Victorian charges, and six months later, in March 2000 – three months after Y2K proved to be as innocuous as Dobbs was nocuous – he was freed. It was another chapter in a long tale of horror. Arrested by NSW Police on the day of his release, he was extradited to Brisbane over the rape of a young girl. This time, investigators were determined he would be sent away for more than six months, and they planned a case that included 335 incidents, many of them individually carrying sentences that would lock him away for years and years. Soon after, Dobbs pleaded guilty and signalled he would assist Queensland Police in their investigations.

The offending by Dobbs blew wide open behaviour that is as old as humanity but which, by the early twenty-first century, had moved from dark rooms to the dark web, a portion of the internet home to depravity and criminality. Paedophilia was uncomfortably common news by the time Dobbs's crimes were discovered. Through decades of peeling away uncomfortable truths, the public had become more alert to the dangers children were exposed to, with communities of paedophiles preying on them just out of plain sight. Parents had long warned their children against stranger danger. They'd warned them about the risks of using public toilets. They'd even warned them to be wary of adults who just seemed too friendly. Yet the offences seemed isolated. But the Wood Royal Commission in New South Wales in the mid-1990s alerted the nation to the scale of the problem and prompted greater scrutiny of havens meant for children. Religious institutions, the Boy Scouts, state orphanages, boarding schools – all would emerge as 'safe places' for paedophiles to fulfil their evil desires, their conduct opaque.

The portability and simplicity of digital technology changed everything. The capturing and sharing of conquests became part of the paedophile's repertoire. Dozens of images became hundreds, even thousands, of images. Filming became as easy as pressing a button on a camera a little bigger than the palm of a hand. Storing movies and catalogues of wickedness became cheap and secure. Sharing them at scale was the next step for offenders like Dobbs who were to harness the rising power of the internet, which was rapidly moving from being a useful but difficult-to-access technology to being an essential tool for every scientific, social and commercial interaction. Want to book a holiday? Go online. Want to buy and sell shares? Go online. Want to wish your friend across the world a happy birthday? Go online. And yes, want to see pornography? Go online. Want to see abusive pornography? Go online. Want to sell abusive pornography? It was all online, in the dark web. And it was all built on the murky foundations established by chronic abusers like Geoffrey Robert Dobbs.

Veteran officers were floored by the breadth of Dobbs's abuse – as the investigation continued, his tally of victims quickly climbed. But it was the evidence that continued to spill out that influenced their work. Dobbs admitted to having offended for about thirty-five years before being caught. All of his crimes brought sickening details: he used objects like pens and carrots to abuse children, hid their pubic hair in canisters, kept young girls' underpants. Early on, he used basic technology to enhance his wicked ways. It was in 1985 – fourteen years before he was caught – that he started videorecording the abuse of children aged from six months to early teens. He carried a camera everywhere: from beaches to shopping malls, change rooms to Brisbane's South Bank, the latter a refuge for families with young children, with its plentiful pools. In one heartbreaking episode, an investigator found images of his own children, playing at South Bank, on Dobbs's camera.

Dobbs hid his camera so that those captured on it remained unaware. He was a polished groomer, wrangling his way into families, churches and community organisations with apparent ease. He held a host of respectable volunteer positions, from an instructor for girls' gymnastics to a Sunday school teacher at one church, and a youth group leader at another; he was also a Scout leader. Ominously, he even followed some children to their parents' vehicles, noting the registration numbers to track them down later. On occasion, his abuse started less than one hour after meeting a child; in one case, the victim's parents believed it happened inside four minutes. The images investigators pored over showed a predilection for photos taken with a long lens of children getting changed and infants in various stages of undress. And perhaps in a sign of what crime fighters would have to deal with just a few years later, some images had been converted from video footage into a form suitable for distribution online.

Dobbs, who had no prior convictions, lived in suburban Brisbane. To those who met him, he appeared a pillar of the community: a god-fearing family man whose volunteer work should be applauded. But in court in 2003, he was revealed as a monster, eventually pleading guilty to more than 100 charges for crimes over three decades, against dozens of identified children. Those charges were broad and included carnal knowledge of children under twelve, maintaining a sexual relationship with a child, indecent dealing, and recording indecent visual images between 1972 and 1999. He also admitted to working with three other paedophiles across the state in an ad-hoc arrangement where victims were shared. His file was stamped with two indefinite life sentences, and no-one thought the man who was widely labelled Australia's worst paedophile would ever be released. That changed in 2015 when those indefinite sentences were commuted to fifteen-year terms, but they were to be served concurrently with life sentences he'd also received. Dobbs remains in jail.[1]

Salvatore Vasta, now a judge in the Federal Circuit Court, was a senior police prosecutor when he was handed Dobbs's file soon after the offender returned to Brisbane. 'He was the game changer,' Judge Vasta says, pointing to the scope of Dobbs's offending, and his ability to groom children and remain undetected for so long. Judge Vasta remembers the case being made more complex by the fact that, while Dobbs had said he would plead guilty, police had been unable to identify dozens of victims. 'We used to wait for people to come to police to make a complaint,' he says, but the Dobbs's case flipped that. 'This was one where police had evidence that offences had taken place, but no complaints, so they had to actually go looking for victims.' It's harrowing to realise that many of those victims, who are now in their twenties and thirties and forties, perhaps even their fifties, have never been found. 'We had never seen anything like this whatsoever,' Judge Vasta says. As police found individual victims, statements were taken from them and handed to him. 'And that's why this was a game changer,' says Judge Vasta. 'The focus wasn't on "Someone's committed a crime, let's arrest him, prosecute him and have him punished". This was about trying to identify victims and ensure they were okay.'

The tally stalled at sixty-two, all children who had never previously come forward to reveal the sordid attacks they'd suffered. Vasta, as a prosecutor, saw a side of human life most of us don't. Dobbs was the worst abuser he had ever encountered. 'When I stopped being a prosecutor and became [a] judge, I kept the schedule of offences with Dobbs. It had been so many hours of my life.'

While the World Wide Web had become publicly accessible about a decade earlier, its use at the time of Dobbs's arrest was still largely restricted to work tasks. Judge Vasta says he remembers querying whether there was any evidence of distribution of images. The answer came back that there was none, and Dobbs was duly sentenced. But a few months later, Sal Vasta answered a call from then sergeant Jon Rouse, from Taskforce Argos. Rouse, who was already making a name for himself both in Australia and globally, had taken a call from Interpol. Vasta ducked down to Rouse's office and found that Dobbs's case had presented a new challenge: evidence of images being trafficked. Dobbs was appearing in videos picked up in another investigation on the other side of the world.

Rouse says the discovery shaped him. Here was a rapist producing images using a concealed VHS handicam. 'How the hell did that get into a global paedophile network?' asks Rouse. Interpol was searching for Dobbs, based on what it had found, but he'd already been arrested in Australia. 'A light bulb went off,' Rouse says. 'I'm this little piss-ant sitting in Queensland, but it taught me that we had a role to play beyond our borders.' How could you know where a tortured and tormented child was until you found her? It was a rhetorical question. And once she was located in another country, did that mean you were not going to help? Another rhetorical question. Rouse knows that borders, in online child sex cases, do not exist.

Judge Vasta says Dobbs provided lessons for both police and the justice system as the use of technology grew: 'We just didn't realise that we had these sorts of networks, that we had people whose desire was actually to offend, record the thing, live it over and over again, and exchange those sorts of things with like-minded people.' The case will always stick in his mind, especially a conversation with the father of two of Dobbs's victims. The man told Vasta that he remembered Dobbs, whom he knew, visiting the family home. He also remembered leaving Dobbs alone with his children, telling the former prosecutor that he was gone for 'no more than four minutes'. Vasta says, 'And we've got two minutes of video showing him [Dobbs] abusing the man's daughters.'

Dobbs's camera was a weapon, but it also served as crucial evidence for police. In more than a few cases, a broken camera was the key to prosecuting an offender early on. But that was the first chapter in a technology story that grew slowly and then erupted, with the dark room giving way to the dark web, that part of the internet haunted by criminals, terrorists and agents of exploitation who have both the means and the will to keep their activities out of plain sight.

•

It started with Internet Relay Chat, which had existed for many years. Investigators started seeing it being used by offenders because it allowed text messages to be delivered to multiple users at the same time. The web portal MSN and the social media sites Myspace and Facebook soon began playing their own part in online child sex abuse. The explosion in mobile technology, including the smartphone and other hand-held devices, provided a wealth of new avenues for child abusers to track down victims. In the last three months of 2010, smartphones outsold PCs worldwide.[2] Soon, the number of online users trading child sex abuse images was growing exponentially. Scarily, at the same time, according to educators, the starter's gun was fired on parents using devices to pacify toddlers.

We all know the rest of the story, especially the proliferation of social media sites and mobile apps which serve as a 24/7 lure for pre-teens and teens, expedited by virtual reality, at least in the short term. But other technologies or distribution channels that are not as publicly well known have also been part of the global technology story. One is peer-to-peer file-sharing, where digital files are shared between people without a server, and another is the dark web – a term that first emerged around the time of the huge growth in smartphone use, although debate surrounds how long it has truly existed.

Understanding the dark web is crucial to understanding the size of the task confronting those waging a war against online child sex abusers. Imagine an iceberg, an image often used to illustrate the tiny part of the internet that sits out in the open, in public view. Underneath is the remainder of cyberspace, called the deep web. Google, Chrome and other traditional browsers do not take you to this part of the web. That doesn't mean it's dangerous; indeed, according to a report on organised crime in Queensland, most of it is 'benign, whether it is hidden deliberately or is simply not indexed due to its unpopularity or web format'.[3] But in the depths of the deep web lies the dark web, accessible only through the use of special programs like Tor, I2P or Freenet. This is where anonymous and often illegal activities are carried out, including 'services offering contract killings and the sale of illegal drugs and weapons'.[4] It's also where online sex abusers indulge themselves, swapping images, trafficking children, offering rape on demand, and building criminal sex abuse networks. The networks are not amateur pop-ups – they are sophisticated operations built like companies, their operations hidden from those not invited in. With Tor, the most commonly used pathway into the dark web, there is no digital footprint, allowing complete anonymity. And the number of users is in the millions.

Just consider the phenomenal speed of recent technology growth. Dobbs used his camera for more than three decades. In 2023, two decades after his conviction, the number of smartphone users sits at 6.92 billion, meaning over 86 per cent of the world's population owns a smartphone.[5] Susan McLean, the former Victorian detective whose services are now sought globally as an online safety educator, says she remembers the first time she spoke on a mobile phone. She was at court, having charged an alleged offender, and 'he handed me this brick thing and said he had talked to his solicitor, and I'm thinking, "What the hell is this?" A crook with his ill-gotten gains could afford a phone when no-one else could!' But within the next decade, McLean would be inundated by requests from schools trying to understand the online challenges facing children.

Another big spike occurred when phone companies offered unlimited texts for free. 'Before that, every time you sent a text message, that was money off your account; if you sent a picture message, that was even more money off your account,' McLean says. And that cost was a 'protective factor' for children because they couldn't afford it.

A former senior officer at the FBI, Arnold Bell, says when he first began work at the bureau, exploitative or abusive material might arrive at someone's doorstep by mail. The risk of interception of this material, given the number of hands through which it passed, was high. 'Now you could sit in your basement and have three monitors and have everything you want pumped into your house,' says Bell. 'And it's encrypted ...'

That growth in technology and predators' use of it pitted police against paedophiles in a new way. Police had to disrupt their traditional practices and chart a different path. That was because criminals not only used technology to advance their crimes but also to avoid detection. Sudden discoveries due to camera repairs became increasingly irrelevant as police established novel covert operations, fought for new laws, swapped information with other countries in a way not previously seen, and established a global victim identification database with millions of images. All these practices are explored in the following chapters, and all have proven highly successful in hunting down evil and rescuing young children.

Without doubt, covert operations headline that success, allowing officers to infiltrate crime networks by impersonating teen girls or middle-aged offenders or savvy online abusers deep inside the dark web. Early on, when technology didn't offer live streaming, it was relatively easy to convince predators that a forty-year-old female officer was a teen. Rouse says officers would study up on teen bands and fashion, magazines, movies and lingo to be able to converse freely with those on the other end of a messaging service. Each undercover agent kept a script next to them, recording what they had said previously so they didn't slip up. 'You couldn't afford not to get it right,' says Rouse. Nowadays, officers term it 'social engineering', but back then it was simply acting. And its success in nabbing wrongdoers means it is still done widely, as resources allow, in 2023.

Rouse gives this example of how it has always worked – and always will. Back in the early 2000s, a Sydney man was intercepted trying to contact young girls in Brisbane. A Queensland police officer had adopted the profile of a teen and she and the Sydney man had agreed to meet. 'This guy flies into Brisbane airport to meet what he thought was a young girl. His plan was to take her to the Sunshine Coast,' Rouse says. NSW Police provided surveillance from the offender's home to the airport, alerting Queensland Police to what he was wearing. In Brisbane, local officers took control of the airport's CCTV cameras and watched the man meet the 'girl': a tiny undercover officer with her blonde hair tucked up under a baseball cap, and carrying a boogie board. Then police pounced.

As mentioned earlier, the number of offenders who are caught is important to Rouse, but his real key performance indicator, or KPI, is the rescue of a child, and undercover agents have proven crucial in doing that. The practice is controversial, and we discuss that later, but investigators in this area widely believe it is impossible to penetrate the dark web without a disguise. Officers will use passwords usually offered up by someone who has been apprehended and is looking for a lesser sentence. Then they play a waiting game, joining users in discussions of child sex offences, sometimes uploading images they've located elsewhere, and gathering as much evidence as they can to close down a network, bring perpetrators to justice, and rescue the children who are being abused.

Older, more traditional ways have not been discarded, though. The best example of this is the United States Postal Inspection Service, which has achieved stellar results stretching back before home computers dominated our lives. In one case, when the internet was still predominantly a business tool, the service seized data listing individuals around the world who had bought access to websites supplying child pornography. More than 389 000 listings were obtained, involving 4700 paedophile websites and

350 000 customers in sixty countries, including Australia. The culprit behind the data received a massive 1335-year sentence in the United States, where he was based.

Each case carries a lesson. Rouse tells of a UK operation where 'only 5 per cent of 3000 arrested had a criminal history. More than 100 children there were removed from sexually abusive situations.' This was in 1999, before any of us were contemplating the reach of online interactions. What it taught crime fighters was that offenders needed to be proactively targeted, and new ways of doing that had to be found. And it emphasised a learning from the Dobbs case, where his images were found in the United States. Child sex crimes, from exploitation to trafficking, don't respect borders, and the worst offenders could be those you least suspect. It was a former Australian police officer, Bernard Keith Hergert, who taught Rouse that.

Hergert was Australia's first 'international victim identification referral', meaning evidence implicating him overseas was sent to Australia, where investigators believed he was located. That referral prompted a new partnership between Australia and the United Kingdom, and a new friendship between Rouse and Paul Griffiths, a global expert in victim identification. In 2002, the UK National Criminal Intelligence Serious Sex Offenders Unit arrested someone over the rape of an eight-year-old. He was found to be in possession of a large quantity of child abuse material, including five CDs. An Australian accent on the recordings stood out, along with specific background scenery. The evidence was packaged up and sent to the AFP in Australia, which sent it to state and territory units. And that's how it fell into the hands of Jon Rouse. This was the start of Australia's story around victim identification, which has increasingly become ground zero for crime fighters desperate to rescue child sex victims. There are two dominant ways in which a child victim is now identified. The first is through huge online databases that chronicle identified and unidentified children who have been spotted in images, with this information made available to investigators around the world. The second is old-fashioned police work where each image is viewed as evidence.

In Hergert's case, it was an accent that led investigators to Australia, and it was then a vehicle, flora and fauna, camping equipment and a watch that all provided clues. It's a long process, requiring enormous patience. In this case, months went by and, in a desperate effort to reach the four-year-old at the heart of the images, the media were called on to help. Soon after, Hergert, from North Queensland, was arrested and a small girl was saved. She had been forced to watch while needles were inserted by her tormentor into her buttocks. Hergert was sentenced to ten years' jail, with a requirement to let authorities know his address for twenty years after his release. Authorities won't release his current whereabouts.

•

Despite the subsequent convictions, the cases of Dobbs and Hergert illustrated a lack of national coordination. No international networks existed then either – in regard to Hergert, there was simply a friendly informal request from the United Kingdom. And there were no protocols in place, or laws that could help officers track down paedophiles.

But Hergert's case showed the importance of treating every single image as an individual crime scene, with single clues being tracked until they could provide a path forward. 'It is the capture of a moment in time when a criminal offence is happening,' Rouse says. 'A child is being raped. You wrap the crime scene tape around that, and start analysing what you've got.' The crucial question is what clues can be extracted from each image? How might the grainy photo of a cushion help, or a slice of curtain in the background? Rarely do offenders show their faces, but a mole on a hand or a mark on a penis can be the clincher in court. Audio can also quickly direct investigators to specific countries or regions, although it's the clue that hardened officers hate: a progression from an image showing a point in time to hearing the excruciating pain of a child being tormented. Sometimes that assault is delivered by a stranger but often by someone the child knows. Most investigators only need to listen to the audio in a case once, because every single sound stays with them.

It would be amiss here not to credit Anders Persson, who served as a Swedish police officer before becoming the team leader for the French-based Interpol victim identification group, for his work in identifying victims. Persson set up a database in Sweden before being drafted to establish the same for Interpol. That resulted in the International Child Sexual Exploitation (ICSE) database, a gigantic library of images that officers around the world can search. Born out of frustration, that database, when it was created, served as the key to a new era of global cooperation. And Australia was at the centre of that.

Persson, now a beekeeper, says the database was a direct response to the tsunami of child sex material flooding the internet at the time. 'We realised that around the world, there were police forces sitting, trying to identify the same images which another country already had identified,' he says. On some occasions, a crime unit would spend months trying to identify a perpetrator, to later find out they had already been jailed in another country. That led Persson to first establish a database in Sweden, as the internet started to take off, but its use was confined to just a few countries. When he later set up ICSE at Interpol, it changed global policing. 'It's like inventing the wheel,' Persson says. As images came to light, officers in any country could search the database to find out whether that image had already been investigated, or whether more images existed of the same victim or perpetrator. The tool's use and content grew exponentially.

Another database called the Australian National Victim Image Library (ANVIL) was set up by Rouse in 2005. It helped in the detection of new images by removing those around the world that had already been identified. Its successor, the Australian Victim Identification Database (AVID), which now sits in the Australian Centre to Counter Child Exploitation (ACCCE) – launched in 2018 to drive a national response to child exploitation – includes every seizure made in Australia: millions of images. Only a tiny portion of those might relate to sex abuse, but the full seizure is uploaded so that investigators have access to details that might only later become important. AVID also feeds into the global database, which focuses on those who have been identified (victims and perpetrators) and those who have not. Both are game changers in the fight to rescue children. And arguably, amid a plethora of contributions,

AVID might serve to be Rouse's biggest contribution because of the power it holds in identifying victims and perpetrators.

Intelligence-led operations are also likely to play a bigger role as predators find new ways to use technology to harm children. Warren Bulmer, an expert in victim identification, came to Australia from Toronto in 2020, having previously worked on many cases with Rouse. He says law enforcement agencies are sitting on a mountain of data, only some of which is used in prosecutions. What remains could be investigated to provide more leads, identity other offenders, and perhaps solve other cases.

These are modern measures to combat a crime that finds new pathways to spread its evil. Persson doesn't believe the world is filling up with more and more paedophiles, but he does think that technology has rampantly increased the ways in which abuse material can be recorded and shared. The camera shop and its repair staff are in the past. 'Today, you have the camera in your mobile phone,' says Persson. 'You film a scene with your camera and you distribute it over the internet with the same camera.' That has killed off some of the old-fashioned policing techniques, knocked down boundaries, and forged a new path where one of the big obstacles is funding. 'But children are the foundation of this society,' Persson says. 'And if we can't take care of them, what can we do?'

3

The wild wild web

They're a century apart, but the experiences of the invention of the automobile and the creation of the internet beg comparison. Both were disruptive technologies that forever changed the way humans had social contact with each other, how they did business, how they spent their money. And their spread – one in the early 1900s, the other in the early 2000s – was fast and irreversible.

They also provide a stark contrast. The car, even in its slow, early-twentieth-century form, required a licence to drive, and adherence to laws written to keep drivers, passengers and innocent bystanders safe. The internet came with no rules and no licensing, only the occasional warning to handle with care – even though it was put in the hands of young, vulnerable, often naive users. Imagine handing the keys of a car to a fourteen-year-old and telling them to take it for a spin, without any guidance. It's a ludicrous idea. But we unthinkingly put online devices into the hands of not just fourteen-year-olds, but sometimes fourteen-month-olds, and let those devices occupy them. Dr Janine Rowse, a forensic physician, says the seatbelts and airbags required in our vehicles by law are aimed at offering protection. 'But online,' she says, 'what are the seatbelts? Where are the airbags? We haven't got that worked out yet.'

Dr Rowse was working as a GP when she became concerned by the number of teens fronting her youth clinic after being sexually assaulted. Many had met their assailant online. It niggled at her. When she discovered that Dr Joanna Tully, a paediatrician and now Deputy Director of the Victorian Forensic Paediatric Medical Service at the Monash Children's and Royal Children's hospitals in Melbourne, held similar concerns based on her work, the two medicos embarked on a study of technology-facilitated sexual assaults involving children. It's a study that should frighten us all.[1]

Of the 515 children who had been sexually assaulted and subsequently examined at just one paediatric forensic medical centre in Melbourne, seventy – or almost 14 per cent – had met their assailant online. This was in the seven years leading up to 2020, and that percentage had risen from 4 per cent in the previous seven years. Some of the children were aged seventeen, but many were only twelve, with the average age being fifteen. Dr Rowse, who is also a parent, says: 'It's absolutely frightening, because you have to run to keep up in this area, and already my eight-year-old who has an iPad, compulsory with school ... she's better at it than I am. And this is what my PhD is in!'

Most of the assaults happened at the first 'contact' meeting. One-third occurred at the offender's home, and another third at a public place, like a park or public toilets. Almost all the victims were female and all the perpetrators were male. Offenders were on average a decade older than their prey, but they ranged up to twenty-six years older, and in some cases had lied about their age. Most of the children lived at home with their parents. The platforms on which the victims and perpetrators met varied, but typically they were the ones favoured by children, including Facebook and Snapchat. Dating apps such as Tinder, Grindr and Skout were other online meeting places.

The study by Rowse and Tully shows but the tiny tip of the iceberg because it only involved those who agreed to take part in the study, accessed the medical centre after being assaulted offline, and whose assault had been reported to police. The assault also had to have occurred 'in a forensically relevant timeframe'. 'Our data just gives you one tiny snapshot of a huge problem,' Dr Rowse says. It also highlights the enormous limitations of the laws that govern its use. How is it that vulnerable children, as young as twelve for example, are freely accessing adult sites? Where are the signals that direct the traffic here? 'I think a lot of people don't want to know about it,' says Rowse. 'They don't want to hear about it. But it can happen to anybody's child.'

Without labouring the analogy, any of our children can also be caught up in a traffic accident. How many parents are gripped with worry when our children, with a huge smile, sit behind the wheel of a car and take off for the very first time? Too many parents have had that knock on the door from a police officer, breaking the news that their child has been involved in a car crash and has been terribly injured, or is even dead. But isn't that what we are seeing now in the online world, with disturbing regularity?

Schoolchildren bullied to the point where they refuse to attend class. Punch-ups captured on video that mar a child's reputation and even follow them from school to school. Isolation that drives loneliness and anxiety and depression. And, in some cases, suicide – when online communication has been used as a weapon to taunt and torment, or when a predator, using online anonymity, preys on a child. But where road safety laws, campaigns and proactive courses evolved as the motor vehicle played an increasingly bigger role in our lives, no matching rigour in rules, education and safety requirements has been applied to online activities. Lawyer Bill Potts takes it further, saying the internet holds more dangers than a motor vehicle. 'That's because the lives lost, the mangling of limbs and mind, are exactly the same,' he says. 'But it's difficult to find who the driver is, or [there's] the fact you've been hit by someone that's not even in this state. [And] It's not something that exists for a moment. It exists for all time.'

Potts is one of Australia's most experienced lawyers and has twice served as president of the Queensland Law Society. He is unapologetic in his assessment of the law and how it misses the technology giants that he says operate unchecked. He explains that, when it comes to online sex abuse, the law is simply 'not fit for purpose', for a host of reasons: the size of Australia when it comes to policing international crime, the difference in laws in different jurisdictions, and the mammoth power wielded by the big social media platforms. Laws in Australia have been hamstrung because of the difficulty in proving where online crimes are occurring, and many countries are 'not playing by our laws'. Potts says, 'We talk about the justice system and we think it's about truth and justice. In fact, it's not about that. It's about proof.'

As a journalist, I've interviewed Potts for more than thirty years and he is usually outspoken but always temperate. This subject – the unchecked dangers presenting online – challenges that demeanour. Potts says some online sexual assaults take place in 'lawless failed states' which have not joined international treaties nor allow extradition. Even at home here in Australia, our laws have failed dismally in addressing the digital age, which largely has meant that online sites have been able to do what they like. Options do exist to rein them in. Potts believes Australia could go further in regulating their activities, to force them to use their algorithms to stop the criminal activity they are hosting. 'This is something that is well within their technology,' he says, 'but we lack the political will.' And what would change that? 'We would need a government with courage, with an eye to the reality of the seriousness of the offending and the harm that is done, to stand up and make an international example stand.' He adds that the consequence of this failure is clear: 'We've essentially got an internet that is devoid of morality, devoid of conscience, and devoid, it seems, of responsibility – and that is a very dangerous thing.'

Sonya Ryan, whose daughter, Carly, was murdered by a sex predator she met online, knows that better than most of us and wants greater controls. 'They should remove all child exploitation off their platforms,' she says. 'They've got the AI technology. I think it's profit and privacy at the expense of our most vulnerable. It's almost like social media platforms give a veil of privacy to criminals.' Here, she's talking about end-to-end encryption, which increases the privacy of conversations but makes it much more difficult for police to access information. In Carly's case, the sexual predator used a fake identification to pretend he was someone else online. 'Fraud is a huge offence offline so why is it possible to fake their identity online?' Sonya Ryan asks. 'We are accountable for our actions offline through law. So why is this happening in the online space and the consequences are not the same as if we were doing it offline?'

Dr Rick Brown, Deputy Director of the Australian Institute of Criminology, says solutions to some of these problems already exist but are not being fully enacted. Offering one example, he says: 'There are all sorts of applications that exist to help with online verification of identity.' Even that would assist in stopping twelve-year-olds from accessing dating sites, or young children joining TikTok. 'Yet, there's been a reluctance for those to be picked up. That's just one example where I think the big companies, social media companies, could do more to deal with these issues.' Dr Brown says the issues around encryption also needed to be more strongly considered because the promised privacy could risk a child's safety. 'Essentially, child safety is being sacrificed for this notion of privacy on the basis that presumably privacy sells more than child safety does,' he says. Communications are carrying greater anonymity, which is sold as greater privacy. But does it then protect those preying on children, and hamper those investigating alleged abuse? Dr Brown says the algorithms used to identify abusive material cannot operate in an encrypted space, and that, in turn, leads to fewer reports of online crimes.

Hetty Johnston AM, who founded the child-protection agency Bravehearts after her daughter's disclosure of sexual assault, believes the definition of online crimes around sex abuse also needs to be changed, and a voice given to victims, especially before the court. Online child sex abuse, she says, should be tried as manslaughter, or even murder in some cases. 'It can just take a long time for that person to actually die.' She says the psychological scars can impact a young victim for years, and some suicide as a teen. 'For my money, that's murder or manslaughter,' she says. Greater and forced regulation of online providers would be a start, but penalties also need to fit the crimes, she says. 'It's very difficult for regulators and legislators to keep up with this. It's like the Industrial Revolution, but it's the technology revolution, and everything is changing so fast.'

Certainly that's borne out by the history of how laws have been applied to online activity and in particular the policing of online child sex abuse. Only twenty years ago, as the internet was exploding like fireworks across the globe, it was difficult to match a law to a crime. Indeed, Jon Rouse remembers taking hardcopies of images to the office of the state government censor, who would then declare it 'illegal content' under laws governing computer gaming and images. 'The image is a crime scene,' Rouse says. 'That's a moment in time when a child was raped. How was that a computer game? How was that not a criminal offence?'

In 2003, under Rouse's advocacy, specific laws were introduced into the criminal code in Queensland. But it was after one specific investigation that other states and the Commonwealth charged ahead with laws aimed at online crime. This was because Operation Auxin, which

THE WILD WILD WEB

is discussed in detail in Chapter 5, provided an almighty wake-up call for parents and policymakers over the extent of online child sex crimes. More than 700 Australians were targeted in that operation, which tied credit cards to a website that provided access to child sex abuse. The business was run out of Eastern Europe, and the FBI handed the list of alleged offenders to Australian authorities. It included teachers and businessmen, police officers and volunteers, childcare operators, public servants and clergymen. Since then, the laws that govern online crime, including child abuse, have been broadened to envelop everything from grooming to authorising the takeover of criminal online accounts, and the right to demand passwords from those allegedly using the web to sexually abuse children.

'The law has been quite adaptive,' Rouse says. But it's like playing a constant game of catch-up as predators find new ways to indulge their crimes. Even in Australia, the law is sensationally inconsistent. For example, covert operations where a police officer adopts the online identity of a child sex abuser are allowed in some states but not in others. The criminal codes are not uniform in the various state and territory jurisdictions. There is no national legislation that umbrellas all crimes. Add to that the international challenges, where different appetites determine laws and punishment, and the result is a kaleidoscope of laws that sometimes work but often don't.

•

Great leaps continue to be made in technology and what it delivers. In many parts of our life, that's welcome. New kitchen appliances make our domestic workload easier. Exercise machines chart our health. Software systems transcribe speech. The list is long. But those same advances herald a bleak future for law enforcement battling the scourge of online child sex abuse. Virtual reality and augmented reality will change the way we use screens. There's the virtual shared space called the metaverse. There's deepfake technology and neural synthesis. Cloud gaming. Wearable haptic suits which deliver feedback to the body in computer games. How will predators use these advances to increase the number and types of assaults they might wage on our children?

Jon Rouse shakes his head. 'If we don't get a handle on that now ...' His voice trails off, then he launches into a series of questions that need answers: 'What's a sexual assault in the metaverse look like? How do we investigate that? What charges would fit?' These concerns are widely shared. Victim identification specialist Paul Griffiths describes it as a 'massive' looming issue: 'The ability to determine whether or not an image is 100 per cent real, the ability to hide identities and to make people think that images are other people ... It's going to be a big problem.' Rouse says investigators know what is coming, but there is no consideration of how it will be policed. He joins the chorus of others – parents, lawyers, victims – who believe part of the solution lies in greater regulation and enforcement. Referring to online platforms, he says: 'They've proven that they can't be responsible with their technology because there are so many children being abused.'

Rouse says other hurdles exist to curtailing online abuse. He, too, is concerned that end-to-end encryption is

THE WILD WILD WEB

further anonymising crimes, making it more difficult for police to do their work. And he points out that the use of facial recognition technology in fighting crime has been outlawed in Australia based on privacy concerns. 'But what about the rights of the child here? I understand the concerns around the potential for misuse, but if you put the correct governance around it and limit access to it ... we should be using it. We haven't had the mature conversation in Australia around this.' He shows me photographs of about sixty young Australian girls, all from online child sex movies, whose identities remain a secret. Apart from fingering offenders, that's where facial recognition technology could make a material difference – helping to recognise the thousands and thousands of children tagged as 'unidentified victims' in police databases.

Paul Griffiths raises the irony around facial recognition technology: 'It's galling that that is such an issue. Who are these people who are so offended that someone's looking for their face when they've quite happily put their face on the internet?' Jim Cole, who recently retired as Supervisory Special Agent with the US Department of Homeland Security, says facial recognition routinely saves children when it is used in his home country. 'Absolutely, 100 per cent,' he says. He adds that he is a strong advocate for the ethical use of artificial intelligence like this, and also asserts he is a 'big believer in privacy'. 'But what about the children's privacy?' he asks. 'What about the victim's privacy? Everybody advocates for privacy, but in that advocacy, it's really all about the offender's privacy. It's not about the victim's privacy, whose images are being shared around the globe. Think about what we're protecting versus what we're failing to protect. It's a child's worst moment. It's sexual abuse. It's the rape of a child ...'

The challenge of combating online sex abuse will always be harder outside our own borders without every country buying in. Online child sex abuse in impoverished countries can be driven by economic needs, with families willing to sell their young children for sex in order to put food on the table. Different cultures also deliver different appetites for different laws. Those factors, and the need to make a dent in the huge global dark web networks, flagged the need to 'disrupt' current models and try new ways of stopping child sex networks, according to former FBI agent Arnold Bell. He says Operation Achilles, a two-year joint investigation that began in 2006 and involved US and Australian teams, and which is detailed in Chapter 6, prompted the use of laws governed by the *Racketeer Influenced and Corrupt Organizations Act* (RICO). Passed in 1970, RICO previously had been used for crimes like illegal gambling, bribery, kidnapping, murder, money laundering, drug trafficking and slavery. 'It's normally used for the Mafia or organised crime groups,' Bell says. 'And what that means is that everyone in the group is culpable regardless of their role.' That means now, a network's administrator and technology assistant, even the person who buys the coffee, are 'equally culpable' if they are part of the crime group.

Rouse believes that type of disruption, as well as switching the focus from offenders to a 'victim-centric approach', are the best ways to make inroads into this wrongdoing that involves millions worldwide. 'It requires us to be a little bit more diverse in our strategy. Disruption has to become a bigger part of what policing is doing and what the community is doing,' he says.

It's a given that different countries require different approaches. Guillermo Galarza is a senior manager at the US-based International Centre for Missing & Exploited Children (ICMEC), which plays a huge role in developing training, advocacy and legal approaches in countries around the world. It also works with educators, researchers and healthcare professionals in impoverished countries in a bid to improve the awareness and policing of child sex crimes. 'Those countries have the same numbers of child exploitation cases, the same victims,' says Galarza. But, he adds, we need to 'really understand what the needs are of some of these developing countries'. Fighting online sex crime has to be fit for purpose.

Georgia Naldrett is the Manager of Stop It Now! Australia, part of The Men's Project at Jesuit Social Services, and a service for those worried about their sexual interest in children. Naldrett says the internet offers an environment for individuals who might never before have committed offences to commit them. 'A perfect example of that is an individual who has no access to children,' she says. 'The internet now offers that environment where it can occur – and it doesn't need to. When we build a playground, we go in and we make sure it's safe for our children to go there. It's built with children's safety in mind. And websites just don't do the same thing. We know children from as young as seven years old are going on social media, on platforms that aren't safe and aren't there to protect them. And so there needs to be a shift in the responsibility of keeping children safe.' The work done by

Australia's eSafety Commissioner was a significant step forward here, says Naldrett.

As Australia's eSafety Commissioner, Julie Inman Grant leads the world's first government regulatory agency committed to keeping its citizens safe online. The safety-by-design principle it embraces requires the big platforms to implement safeguards at the concept stage, not retro-fit them, as has been the case for a long time. This initiative has involved consultation with 180 stakeholders and has now been downloaded by companies in fifty-two countries – it was even lauded by US President Biden in a State of the Union speech. eSafety has also had a string of successes in both the legislative and education arenas. Its scope is huge, covering prevention through research and education, protection through regulatory schemes and inventions, and forging what it calls 'proactive and systemic change'.

Yet the challenges posed online continue to grow, and in many cases, the big companies just ignore all calls to heel. Paul Griffiths says the assistance the big platforms give to investigators varies widely. 'A lot of the problem is that most of these companies are just that – companies. The lawyers have far too much say over what they can do and what they will do,' he says. Inman Grant says end-to-end encryption and the lack of responsibility displayed by some companies are two of the issues that keep her awake at night. She says that, in some cases, the companies aren't even implementing what they have created, or as she puts it, 'eating their own dog food'. And she is calling them out, publicly.

So what else can Australia do? Other countries, such as China, have put strong fences around online use, haven't they? It's a question I pose to Inman Grant. 'I wouldn't ever want to compare us to China because we do all of this according to statutory thresholds around levels of harm,' she responds. 'We have to have regard for free speech and a range of human rights and balance those. China are blunt force censors. They'll shut the internet down. I have to go after pieces of specific content. I'm not blocking entire sites or domains, unless there is what we call an online crisis event.'

•

The history of child abuse, as with most crimes, shows that the law-breakers usually stay ahead of the law-makers. Australia's response to contact abuse, mainly in institutions, for example, has taken decades to reach its current standards, unfortunately denying justice to victims whose lives have been permanently harmed. Still, the responses are happening. In the 1990s, Australia took the lead in legislating to penalise its citizens for leaving the country for the purpose of abusing children in nations such as Indonesia, Thailand and the Philippines; many of those offenders were sentenced to life in prison. And the lessons learned inform today's law-makers, who continue to struggle with limited power over the internet platforms that host sexual violence against children.

This is not just an Australian problem. Jim Cole says the same debate is taking place in the United States, where the law provides the big social media companies with a degree of immunity. He gives the analogy of a multi-hectare amusement park where sex offenders are allowed to freely roam and abuse children. He says in the real world, there would be a very different response – the park owner would be held responsible. 'In the virtual space, we don't hold the same rules or accountability,' he says.

So if our regulatory authority is doing everything it can with the power it has, perhaps it comes back to the laws available to investigators. Rouse says sex abusers need to know that investigators are swarming every platform, and they will use the tiniest mistake – backed by law – to pin down the perpetrators. 'We're now in 2023 and it's still the wild wild web,' he says. 'And it's getting worse, it is absolutely getting worse. The algorithms that they're now using to basically keep our children on devices and going down rabbit holes that can feed them information, [are] really damaging. It's time for the world to get together and say, "Enough."'

That would take an almighty fine dance, because every country has a different view on regulations and laws and enforcement around social media, not to mention the penalties – a point made by former FBI agent Arnold Bell, who has worked with Australia on big global investigations. He says the United States has handed out strong penalties, often without parole, to online child sex offenders, while other nations have sent them away for between two and five years, only to later see them reoffend. 'And there seems to be much more concern about the wellbeing of the perpetrator than of the kids. And that just frosts me to this very day.'

Part 2

Game changers

4

Jon Rouse and Taskforce Argos

Jon Rouse was walking through the offices of Taskforce Argos, the dedicated Queensland police unit focused on the sexual exploitation of children, when a phone call pierced his thoughts. 'Taskforce Argos,' he answered. Silence. 'Hello. Hello.' More silence, stretching perhaps for a minute, or even two. But something told Rouse not to hang up. This wasn't a prank call. And then, a tiny noise. Perhaps a sob. Definitely a sob. It grew louder. 'I'm here whenever you're ready,' Rouse said. 'Just take your time.'

It was 2002, and Rouse had taken over Taskforce Argos's venture into online child sex crimes a year earlier. It was a small unit, with not even a handful of officers, that fed into a larger unit where the focus was squarely on the institutionalised sex crimes that had destroyed the lives of many: churchgoers, Scouts, young students. The taskforce was named after the Greek mythological figure Argos, the all-seeing giant, guardian and protector, strong – always watchful.

Eventually, the voice at the end of the phone became clearer. Haltingly. Slowly. Between tears. It was a man. Rouse guessed he was almost fifty years of age. He'd lived in an orphanage as a very young child. And on weekends, he told Rouse, the groundsman would take boys who lived there to the drive-in, as a 'treat'. There, boldly, without shame, he would brutally rape them. The man on the other end of the phone, hanging on, was a victim himself, and he told Rouse how he had worked up the courage to tell the nuns who had run the orphanage.

A deep breath – Rouse's, not the caller. He pauses the story to tell me: 'And they beat his feet until they bled.' Rouse falls silent, then takes another big breath and explains that the nuns either didn't believe the young boy or didn't want to believe him. The boy was told that he was tarnishing the reputation of a good, upstanding man.

Rouse said what he could, which wasn't much. But the man who made that phone call more than twenty years ago will never know the influence he had on someone who became one of the world's top crime fighters. The man's story was so painful to hear, his life destroyed by a sick predator who was protected by those who were charged with looking after young, vulnerable children. It changed Jon Rouse.

This victim's story spilled out long after the assaults had occurred, but it prompted Rouse to create his own story, which would unfold almost immediately. From a focus on the past, his work would now focus on the future. He couldn't help this man, whose life had been stolen before it had really begun. The man's tormentor was dead. Those who had run the orphanage had taken his accusations – and their denials – to their graves, too. 'I felt I couldn't do a damn thing for him,' Rouse says. 'His whole life has been this disaster because of what happened to him as a young child.' In that moment, Rouse was heartbroken, but in the years since, he's seen the incident – as with the abduction and murder of Daniel Morcombe in 2003 – as a reason to fight harder, to look for new ways to disrupt the old ones. If he can catch paedophiles and stop the abuse when a child is young enough, they might not travel down the same path as this man did. Explaining the contrast with a killing, Rouse says, 'Homicide, you can't fix it. All you can do is try to bring justice to the victim.' He wanted hope, not heartache. He wanted to turn from the utter agony of what had happened in the past, to what would happen in the future. He wanted to use technology to race ahead of the predators who had begun to use it to seek out new victims, young people like the man on the phone had once been.

That phone call would remain top of mind for Jon Rouse for the next two decades as he eschewed promotion, arrived at work as early as 4 a.m., and advocated for new laws to catch new criminals. He would build a team lauded by Interpol and the FBI, coordinate global operations to bring networks of paedophiles to account, and navigate novel ways of policing that pitted new uses of technology against the digital path taken by sex abusers. And every time he boarded a plane, to pick up an award in New York or present at an Interpol conference in France, he would remember the voice of that anonymous middle-aged man and hope he'd found some sense of peace as he climbed into old age.

Three years after the phone call, in 2005, Rouse was still largely unknown on the international stage, but then he was asked to present to 200 other investigators at an Interpol conference in Lyon, France. This was an annual gathering where global experts would nut out new strategies to combat a crime that appeared to be multiplying each day. Rouse was scheduled to talk about the cases of Geoffrey Robert Dobbs and Bernard Keith Hergert (detailed in Chapter 2), the results of which were being lauded internationally. He had a few other cases up his sleeve, too, which other nations were not aware of, where Australia had arrested the perpetrator. Rouse's underlying aim with the presentation was that he wanted paedophiles to come up against not just global expertise, but a global team.

In the audience that day was Daniel Szumilas – now a Detective Chief Inspector attached to Germany's central criminal investigation agency – who had been working in the field for years, wired in with other investigators who understood the enormous challenges the internet was presenting to online sex abuse crime fighters. Szumilas had seen posts on international forums that related to Taskforce Argos, but he didn't know Jon Rouse from Australia. He watched Rouse walk to the stage slowly, tentatively even. 'And I won't ever forget it,' says Szumilas. 'He was very humble, and he said, "I'm Jon from faraway Australia and I've brought a video from Australia to show you."' Szumilas almost laughs, remembering that he thought it might be akin to him bringing up an image of Oktoberfest to introduce Germany. No doubt others thought the same. And then Rouse started the video.

Steve Irwin, the Australian conservationist and television personality, filled the screen. This was the year before Irwin died after being injured by a stingray in Far North

Queensland, and at the time he was probably our most famous Australian. He was everywhere, with that big toothy grin and wide-open eyes. His television series *The Crocodile Hunter* was off the charts in popularity, reaching more than 500 million people in more than 130 countries. And there he was on the screen, in this room in France, with his signature khaki shirt and broad Aussie accent. 'G'day,' he said. 'I'm Steve Irwin.' He told the gathered investigators that he went by the name of The Crocodile Hunter, then said: 'I deal with predators. Big apex predators. Crocodiles. Sharks. Venomous snakes. Virtually any animal that can kill and eat you is my forte. And those predators need my help – unlike the predators that you've got to deal with.' With Irwin uttering those few sentences, Rouse had everyone in the room sitting on the edge of their seat. 'As a parent, and on behalf of all the parents of the world,' continued Irwin, 'we'd like to say thank you very, very much for coming together for this forum on paedophiles, the predators of the world that need to be stamped out, that need to be eliminated.' At this point, Irwin, displaying his idiosyncratic style, looked as though he was about to squash a cockroach. 'By crikey, we sure appreciate that you are doing that. So without further ado, I'd like to introduce to you a really good mate of mine, a fair dinkum Aussie bloke, Jon from the Queensland Police Service, which is in my backyard.'

No surname, just Jon. Steve Irwin ended his introduction with a 'Woo-hoo. Crocs rule mate.' The audience loved it. Rouse now approached the lectern to put Taskforce Argos at the centre of the global fight against online child sex predators. 'It totally blew me away,' Szumilas says. 'He was very very impressive.' Afterwards, Szumilas and a colleague grabbed a bite to eat at Interpol's cafe. Rouse was there, sitting alone at a table. Szumilas remembers him in that moment as he knows him now, eighteen years later: understated, perhaps even a touch closed off at first, but passionate. And above all, committed to saving children.

•

Jon Rouse was born on Papua New Guinea's Manus Island in 1963. His father, Patrick, was an officer in the Royal Australian Navy who rose to the status of commander, picking up an MBE before his retirement in 1978. His mother, Susan, was a naval nurse. The family, including Rouse's two brothers, Greg and Jason, spent many years travelling: Jervis Bay in New South Wales; Singapore; Frankston in Victoria; Canberra. Life on a naval base had its upside, but for Jon it was hard to make friends, and to find the geographic spot where a sense of belonging prevailed. Music was his constant and reliable companion. He'd started tinkering with his mother's Yamaha organ in Singapore, even having lessons, but he preferred to learn by listening. And he loved that he could take his music everywhere, a foundation for a childhood that kept moving house. Eventually, home became Brisbane, where he completed Year 12 at Marist College in Ashgrove. He started learning classical music in Year 10, which led to playing at church services, and then, with The Knack's *My Sharona* stealing the pop-music charts, the idea formed to create a band to play at school events across the city.

Career-wise, however, it was nursing or the police force that topped the list. A two-day work-experience stint in palliative care turned Rouse towards the police uniform, but his interest ebbed and flowed. Needing money to fund his music endeavours, he soon found a job at the Commonwealth Bank in Paddington, in inner Brisbane. Twice there, he had a gun pointed at him. That seems a plain enough sentence, but anyone who has been subjected to an armed robbery will tell you the impact can run for years. Rouse's response, in those moments of terror, was that of a police officer. He lay on the ground, silently reciting what the armed bandit was wearing. In one of the hold-ups, he jumped the counter in a bid to capture the registration number of the getaway vehicle. He remembers two police officers arriving at the bank later that day, carrying their own typewriters, to take his statement. It wouldn't be long before he was wearing the same uniform.

Music remained close by Jon's side. In the 1980s he joined a band, Neon Park (which later branched out into two bands, Hot Sauce and The Electric 80s Show), and toured as support to the likes of Pseudo Echo, Eurogliders, Goanna, The Party Boys, Kevin Borich, and Kids in the Kitchen. In 1984, Rouse joined the Queensland Police Service as a probationary constable – some nights he'd play in his band and then head to class the next day. Late that year, on a rainy afternoon, he joined thirty-odd other males and just two females in graduating. He was probationary police officer P84C19, and he was twenty-one years old.

All young Queensland police recruits are rotated through different units for experience. In Rouse's case, he started at a busy city station before joining some suburban stations, followed by a lengthy stint at the inner-city watch house. But it was at mobile patrols, where each officer had a partner and did an eight-hour shift in a patrol car, that he came to really understand the culture of loyalty around police work. Later, Rouse would be posted to the Criminal Investigation Branch, where seedy drug deals, homicides and thefts filled a hectic schedule, but it was while Rouse was working at mobile patrols that Lance Vercoe became his best mate.

Vercoe, who retired in 2022 after forty-two years as a police officer, actually first met Rouse while the former was working undercover. It was when Rouse still worked at the Commonwealth Bank, and Vercoe, also a keen musician, frequented his gigs with other friends. No-one knew about Vercoe's real job. 'They knew I joined the police,' he says, 'but then I just told them after twelve months [that] I'd had enough and left and that I was just working in various hotels around Brisbane carrying kegs and serving beers.' Vercoe was, in fact, living out of a caravan, having joined a gang whose headline activity was breaking into houses. You can hear the amusement in Vercoe's voice as he describes Rouse back then: 'Jon was very straight up and down the line. I think he was somewhat disgusted about who I was.' In 1985, a year after Rouse graduated, the pair met up again, this time as law enforcement officers, and they later spent four years as mobile patrol partners. 'You had absolute total trust in each other,' Vercoe says. 'You would spend eight hours a day driving around the streets of Brisbane going to the stuff that frontline police officers do: suicides, armed robberies, sieges and brawls.'

One night, they were alerted to the suspicious activities of three men on motorbikes, and having arrested two of them, Vercoe went to arrest the third. 'He was massive, six foot five,' Vercoe says. 'The next thing I know I'm being swung around like a ragdoll. I was in real strife. This guy is a big unit and he was not happy. And next thing I hear this pitter patter of little feet running across the road. Jon launches himself onto the back of this guy and put him into a headlock, which we would call a vascular neck restraint, and it was a technique that they used in the watch house to resolve issues so nobody got hurt. He was like a little bull terrier hanging onto a massive animal [Rouse is small in stature] and he would not let go.' Eventually the man dropped to one knee, and Rouse rolled off him and returned to the car to complete paperwork. Few words were exchanged – he'd done his job. 'He was fearless,' Vercoe says.

In 1995, Rouse's only child, a daughter, was born three months premature – she was tiny, weighing just 700 grams. A year later, having been promoted to detective sergeant, Rouse started working in the Child Abuse Unit. It wasn't his first choice. Or his second choice. Or his third. All day, he'd watch traumatic vision of children being abused and hurt by those who should love them most. The first time was probably the worst: a toddler, lying on her back, sucking a lollipop while being raped by an adult male. Rouse felt sick – an Australian offender, with an Australian child. He went home and hugged his own daughter a touch tighter. Over the next few years, Rouse worked in different policing areas, but all of them focused on crimes against children. In 2001, he was asked to develop a policing model for Taskforce Argos, which had been set up four years earlier, that could take on a new and grubby brand of child sex crimes, those aided and abetted by technology. Vercoe says

Rouse was the perfect candidate because he was internet-savvy, having developed his band's webpage in 1997, and enjoying computer gaming and writing HTML. He also was clearly drawn to protecting children wherever he could.

Inspector Annie Macdonald APM thought that, too. Now retired, she was then Rouse's boss and also ran a small, covert police team attached to the child abuse unit. 'The internet was taking off, and I knew I wanted to have Taskforce Argos do online abuse of children,' she says. Rouse was her only candidate: 'He had drive. Ambition. And the X factor.' The X factor, she explains, was 'want': 'He wanted Taskforce Argos to succeed in the covert operations area. He wanted to make a difference. He wanted it to have integrity and honesty, to be world's best.' Images of child abuse were popping up online, and Macdonald was drawn to the multiplication factor attached to them. 'In every single one of those images,' she says, 'a child has been abused, and every time the same image of the same child is shown to someone else, or bought by someone else, that child was being abused again. So the child could be abused millions of times even though the actual abuse only took [place] the once.' Macdonald knew Rouse would also be onside with the power undercover work could bring to this new area of policing. 'You can imagine the amount of people who laughed at us,' she says. But both Macdonald and Rouse considered covert stings the investigative tool that would nab online offenders. Rouse had the job of setting up the framework, one that has now endured for more than two decades and is being copied elsewhere.

'The only way to catch these [predators] is to portray them,' says Macdonald. 'You can't catch people who are trading this abhorrent vision online unless you become one; you make out that you are one. We had to make sure that what we did was beyond reproach.' A single slip-up would be costly. It was sickening on a day-to-day level, as each image needed to be captured and then classified. 'We would sit there with buckets beside us,' says Macdonald.

Bob Atkinson AO APM knows this world like the back of his hand. He was one of the six royal commissioners appointed in January 2013 to the Royal Commission into Institutional Responses to Child Sexual Abuse. He also served as Queensland police commissioner for twelve years, until his retirement in 2012. He says the internet came at policing like 'the introduction of the aeroplane or the motor vehicle, where it just burst onto the scene, and it just exploded'. Its pace and acceleration were dramatic, particularly for law enforcement personnel who historically were used to boundaries. 'Now all of a sudden, there were no boundaries,' says Atkinson. 'It wasn't just no boundaries nationally. It was no boundaries worldwide. So that was a whole new dimension.'

By 2001, Atkinson had built up a relationship with the FBI. Terrorism, which hit hard with the September 11 attacks, was finding a home online too. But from day one, he knew Rouse would have Australia punching above its weight in the global online sex abuse field. 'All of us have an ability to do things that others wouldn't,' he says, with his signature humility. 'So me personally, I don't think I could work in a children's hospital or in palliative care. I'm not sure that I could work in an aged care home either. But there are people who are a fit for things. And Jon Rouse was clearly a fit for this.' Atkinson says that, in addition to this fit, a leader in this field needs three qualities: knowledge, or the ability to acquire it quickly; energy, commitment and dedication; and recognised integrity and credibility. 'There's been thousands of books written about leadership, but you know it when you see it, and you know it when you don't see it. And Jon Rouse has it.'

It's difficult to find someone who disagrees with this assessment. Even those who've come up against Rouse's take-no-prisoners approach acknowledge his tenacity, passion and commitment to children. 'There's no froth and bubble about Jon,' says Bravehearts founder Hetty Johnston. 'He's serious about protecting kids and there's not even a little nano inch to move either way.' Australian eSafety Commissioner Julie Inman Grant says Rouse has a 'dogged determination to save children'. She thinks 'he's made many sacrifices to his personal mental and physical health. He's just totally driven.' 'He is one of a kind,' says Anders Persson, who is known as 'the father of victim identification' for his work at Interpol. Persson says Rouse put Australia on the map when it comes to tracking down online paedophiles, and his uncanny ability to lead and encourage cooperation between nations meant an untold number of predators have been stopped, and children saved. Rouse understood something that many investigators in other areas didn't: boundaries might exist in the fight against terrorists, drug lords and money launderers, but they had no place in the fight to protect children. 'He's about saving kids,' says former senior FBI agent Arnold Bell. 'He's never been a career-focused guy.'

Bell is right. Rouse told friends he was 'gutted' when a promotion took him away from Taskforce Argos. He fought it by starting work in the Argos office at 5 a.m. and then moving onto his newly assigned tasks at 8 a.m. Inman Grant says Rouse was at his lowest when he was transferred out of Argos, despite the average tenure of officers working on this type of crime being only six months. But soon Rouse was back at his old desk. He'd also developed a reputation for 'managing up', Bell says. 'He'll tell leaders, regardless of rank, what's on his mind.'

•

Rouse's life as a crime fighter would make a popular series on any of the streaming networks whose lifeblood is crime dramas that make heroes of the detectives who always catch their prey. It is truly needle-in-a-haystack investigative work, traversing borders and using high-tech gear to catch often unlikely suspects, helped by occasional strokes of God-given good luck. Few predators ever see Rouse. He's never at the 'busts' that bring them down, nor in court to see them condemned to a deserved fate. By nature he's not a big-noter, so it would be out of character for him to engage in high-speed car pursuits or knock down doors. He speaks with a copper's precision, careful not to give away anything that might compromise an investigation. Even angry, I'd imagine him mild in tone, despite the fact that his nickname amongst police friends worldwide – as well as in his band – is 'Angry'. It's just the way he looks. ICMEC's Guillermo Galarza tells the story of how a colleague asked him about Rouse at a conference, pointing out how angry he looked. 'I said, "That's his nickname!"' says Galarza. 'It's a controlled anger. He's a doer. He's been out in the front line. He's seen the worst of the worst, so when you have to develop that sort of thick skin, you don't have room for politicians just to go in another direction.' Galarza is not the only person to explain that Rouse will tell anyone up the line exactly what the situation is, that he doesn't care too much for niceties. But always, whether it's to a predator, a police boss or a politician, he'll speak at the same even pace and the same volume, showing the character that underpins the method he has brought to his policing.

Rouse is applauded across the globe, perhaps more so than in Australia. 'Jon is a legend in this space,' says Lianna McDonald, Executive Director of the Canadian Centre for Child Protection (C3P). 'He was a pioneer in this space.' She says Rouse has a 'magic sort of recipe' that meant his personality, grit, tactics and intelligence made him a star in this field. 'He doesn't have a bunch of ego. He's just very sensible.' Jim Cole, who worked with the US Department of Homeland Security for more than twenty years, says: 'The world owes Jon a great debt of gratitude. There are children across the globe who are no longer suffering in silence and sexual abuse, because a nameless, faceless figure has basically dedicated his life to pulling them out of that.' Cole says Argos punches well above its weight internationally. 'I think that Taskforce Argos is probably the best child exploitation investigations unit in the world.'

When Rouse started Taskforce Argos's online chase, it was made up of four officers, including himself. Now it has forty staff, amongst them world-class crime fighters who head Interpol groups; train other operatives, including at the FBI; write textbooks; and present at closed, elite conferences. Paul Griffiths, for example, is Taskforce Argos's Victim Identification Manager. He and Rouse worked on an international operation in 2005, and four years later Griffiths moved to Australia to join the unit. 'Once you know that someone is out there abusing kids and putting those images online and you can do something about it, it's very hard to say, "I'm going to go and do something else,"' Griffiths says. Warren Bulmer similarly moved to Australia to join the online paedophile hunt in 2020, first at the ACCCE and now at ICMEC. And Adele Desirs, who spent years in France with Interpol, also came to Australia a few years ago. Here, Rouse has continued to write the script as investigators track down sex offenders. Since the ACCCE was set up in Brisbane, Rouse has moved to provide advice and guidance before his mandatory retirement takes effect this year.

Retirement, however, won't mean slowing down. Rouse's work with Interpol will continue, as will his role as an ambassador for child safety organisations like the Daniel Morcombe and Carly Ryan foundations. As the recipient of four Commissioners Certificates for operational leadership, two excellence awards for Child Protection Prevention, the Queensland Police Medal, the National Service Medal, the Exemplary Conduct medal and the National Police Medal, in addition to the Champion for Children Award from ICMEC and being named 2019 Queenslander of the Year, Rouse will keep his attention focused on children. His next decade of work will be directed at two goals: bringing the big social media platforms to heel, and fighting for victims to have a voice.

Cilla Wallin, Rouse's wife, has a good understanding of his work. The couple met in Sweden in 2014, when Cilla's focus was also online child abuse, although her career trajectory was slightly different from that of her husband's. She says she always wanted to be a mother and an artist, and had two sons, in 1992 and 1994. But it was hard to make a living from art, and so, she says, 'I became a bus driver.' Later, gaining her Master of Laws involved studying online child abuse material. 'And that's when I realised what I wanted to do,' she says. She reviewed Swedish cases and eventually, in 2015, she moved to Lyon to work as an intelligence officer for Interpol. In 2020, just before COVID struck, Cilla finally landed in Australia via Bangkok and Singapore to live with her husband, the pair having married the previous year. Now she reviews safety material and creates and delivers training across Asia – in India, Thailand, Malaysia, Vietnam and Laos – to police officers investigating online sex abuse, which involves changing practices and mindsets. Cilla says Rouse's long work hours are driven by his determination to save children.

At home, Rouse likes having solitary time, away from crowds, with his passions encompassing his wife and daughter, the family's cavoodles, and *Star Wars*. He says he's viewed the original movie at least forty times. 'I remember the first time, I was just blown away by the film. It was like nothing I'd ever seen before,' he says. That, in part, explains the Imperial Star Destroyer, R2-D2 and lightsaber on display at home. It might also explain the names of Cilla and Jon's cavoodles: Chewie and Leia.

'Jon Rouse is one of my heroes, an absolute stellar man,' says Sonya Ryan. She says Rouse pushes aside his own trauma, from a career that's required him to swim through a tsunami of sickening images, in a bid to rescue children. 'That takes a special human being. There are very few people in the world who can do what Jon has done in his career. He is a champion for our children. A champion.'

5

The danger next door

The abduction and murder of Daniel Morcombe, a thirteen-year-old Queensland teenager, just three weeks before Christmas in 2003, changed so much about how we go about our daily business. Few Australians who remember that Christmas will ever forget the fear in the eyes of Daniel's mother, Denise, or the heartbreak writ large on the face of his father, Bruce. This was something that happened in other countries, in big unknowable cities, not on Queensland's Sunshine Coast. The disappearance of Daniel, while he was waiting for a bus to go grab a haircut and complete his Christmas shopping, made a mark in time. It launched a national debate about safety, filled talkback radio airtime, and gave parents the impetus to teach their children about the dangers that lurked where we might least expect them. An open road, near home, didn't feature on too many parental risk registers, but the realisation that the breakdown of a bus and the failure of another to pick up a child altered that. Buses, from then on, were required to collect waiting children regardless of the circumstance.

Parents, from then on, thought of Daniel when they set their children loose on the world.

Fast-forward seven months, to July 2004, and Jon Rouse had set up an office in the Maroochydore Criminal Investigation Branch operations room, just a few kilometres from where Daniel was last seen. His job was to coordinate a series of raids fanning out across the Sunshine Coast to apprehend and question targets in the investigation of a sophisticated online child sex exploitation racket that could be traced all the way back to Belarus in Eastern Europe. A map sat in front of Rouse and his team, which was not unusual – in any police operation of that size, you needed to be exact: the right address at the right time. What struck Rouse and the other officers in that small war room was the number of targets who lived close to where Daniel was last seen. Could one of these suspects in an online child sex racket, whose names were on the list in front of Rouse, also be responsible for Daniel's disappearance? More than ninety officers, divided into twenty teams, set out to knock on the doors of twenty separate residences.

Some of those officers were attached to Taskforce Argos, while others belonged to Operation Vista, which had been set up in the wake of Daniel's disappearance. They were all looking for clues to solve a crime that still dominated daily conversations. More personnel were roped in to boost the team's numbers and experience. 'We were seven months in at this point, with this little boy still missing, and then we get all this information and we don't know about any of these people,' Rouse says. 'We were looking for anything that we could jump on. Anything.' Briefings were scheduled for 5 a.m., which was when officers were given their

instructions before the cacophony of door knocks timed for
6 a.m. Rouse doesn't admit to being nervous at the time but
says he felt hypervigilant. A list of known sex offenders on
the Sunshine Coast, drawn up by the police unit looking at
Daniel's disappearance, along with Rouse's list of cleanskin
targets suspected of involvement in an international online
sex exploitation racket, all of them living in such a confined
area, took everyone by surprise.

The online investigation known as Operation Auxin that
enlivened Argos started with a target list of 706 Australians
that arrived at the Australian High Tech Crime Centre,
hosted by the AFP in Canberra. It was drawn up by US
investigators looking at the use of credit cards tied to a
website that provided access to child sex abuse material.
A company called Regpay Co., Ltd in Belarus, which ran
a global internet pornography business, had thousands
and thousands of paid memberships relating to dozens of
websites featuring children. As well as operating several
of its own websites, the company also earned millions of
dollars by processing credit card fees for more than fifty
other websites. While the Regpay websites were operated
from Belarus, they were hosted by other companies,
including some in the United States. As the probe continued,
US investigators found a huge consumer market, with tens
of thousands of customers around the world, and feared that
some of those using the subscription service might also be
abusing children. The more than 700 Australians were now
in the frame after credit cards in their names were linked to
that website providing access to child sex abuse material.
They had been picked up in Operation Falcon, whose
investigators trawled through 95 000 leads, with lists of

suspects then sent to France, Spain, Britain and Australia. That had launched Operation Auxin in Australia.

In fact, US investigators had passed on details of 1700 Australia-based transactions, as well as suspects' names, addresses, credit card numbers, the specific site that had been accessed, and the date and time when that had been done. As Rouse scanned the list, he thought to himself, How could so many of them live within a stone's throw of where Daniel Morcombe disappeared? Could one of these names hold the key to the disappearance of a teen boy who the nation now held close to its heart? This could be the game changer, the tiny step that would lead investigators to find Daniel, who was still missing.

Rouse had met Denise Morcombe after a speech he'd given. He'd ended it by telling his audience that police did this work to prevent a case like Daniel's from happening again. A woman then came up to him in tears and thanked him – he found out later it was Denise Morcombe. He met Denise again, and her husband, Bruce, when they visited police headquarters to sell red wristbands, trying to do everything they could possibly do to keep their son in the headlines and at the top of people's minds. Rouse bought one and slipped it on his wrist. 'I don't know if I made a commitment to myself then or very soon after that,' he says, 'but I decided it was never coming off until he'd been found. And it didn't.' Taskforce Argos didn't take the lead in the Daniel Morcombe investigation, but given the big crossover between those who offend online and offline – experts say it's as high as 80 per cent – investigators wanted to know if one of the names on that list from America, of those suspected of being paying customers in a child sex abuse racket, might have played a part in Daniel's disappearance. So it was Daniel that every one of those ninety-three police officers had on their minds on that July 2004 morning, as they divided into groups of four and five and set out to knock on doors.

It was Brett Peter Cowan who in 2014 would be sentenced to life in jail for Daniel's abduction and murder. He had not appeared on Rouse's target list from the United States. Perhaps that's a telling sign that sex abuse in our communities is much more pervasive than we might think. That same notion was raised during the investigation into the disappearance of three-year-old William Tyrrell in the NSW town of Kendall in 2014. In that case, which remains unsolved, police also expressed surprise at the number of sex offenders in the area, and they cracked a large child exploitation network where online videos of abuse were allegedly shared.[1]

Ken King remembers Cowan's name appearing on the list of known sex offenders on the Sunshine Coast that was drawn up soon after Daniel Morcombe was reported missing. King, a former Victorian senior constable who now runs a tech start-up, had moved to Queensland the previous year and worked in uniform for eighteen months before taking up a plain-clothes police position on Taskforce Argos. 'When police bring resources to bear into a major incident room, they'll gather people from different stations and squads,' he explains. King was paired up with a colleague and instructed to 'run out the alibis' of those on a list he'd been given: could they prove where they were early on the afternoon of 7 December 2003? He would then take that information, check it thoroughly, and if it proved correct and unsuspicious, the person in question would be removed from the list. If the person couldn't prove where they'd been, or lied about their whereabouts, they would be ranked amongst those considered a person of interest, or POI. 'We went out to Cowan's home address and made two visits in the end,' says King. 'We went to check his alibi too.' King remembers the exact words he said to his partner once they'd left Cowan's home and climbed back into their police car: 'If he's not ripe for that, he's ripe for something else.' His partner, King says, was about to say the same.

As well as driving specific distances to confirm travel times, King and his partner also checked a host of other factors. On one occasion, when Cowan was at work, King crawled under his vehicle to take high-resolution photographs of tyre tracks in case that later became useful. Another time, they again visited Cowan's home to talk to his wife. 'By the end of the process, over a couple of days, we had a guy who had a history of serious offending of this type who had a gap in his alibi,' says King. That gap was thirty to forty minutes, in addition to which, Cowan – as King remembers it – put himself on the road that would've taken him past Daniel Morcombe. He also resembled one of the sketches drawn up by police. King and his partner handed all this information to the lead team and moved on to the next investigation.

By the end of the raids conducted seven months later, on 8 July 2004, thirteen arrests had been made on the Sunshine Coast, on 1346 charges relating to the international online sex exploitation racket. This was just stage one of a national offensive, the raids brought on by the urgency of trying to solve the case of a missing boy. Launching them on the

Sunshine Coast also served as a litmus test for the rest of the country – they could be sold as part of the investigation into Daniel Morcombe without raising the suspicion of the hundreds of others who appeared on the target list provided by US investigators. But at the end of the day, no-one went home buoyed by the arrests. They were no closer to finding Daniel.

Brett Peter Cowan would later be targeted in a major undercover sting that began when a covert officer sat next to him on a flight to Perth. That operation saw Cowan involved in crime scenarios that included bribery and trafficking weapons and even blood diamonds from Africa.[2] Cowan later made admissions about Daniel's abduction and murder. It was almost eight years after Daniel's disappearance that Cowan was arrested, with several more years then passing as the case against him wound its way through the courts.

Rouse remembers being on stage with his band, playing at a ball where the partygoers were made up almost entirely of emergency services and police personnel, when all of a sudden Police Commissioner Bob Atkinson made an announcement. The wristband Rouse had put on years earlier had faded in colour and was now held together by old staples, but at last, Daniel Morcombe's alleged killer had been arrested.

•

While other states made their own decisions over the timing of Operation Auxin, Queensland's second phase occurred two months after the initial raids, in early September 2004.

Over two days, eleven teams of police – a total of forty-nine officers – were deployed to addresses across Queensland, including Cairns, Townsville, Sarina, Proserpine, Mackay and Mount Isa. That resulted in sixteen arrests on 108 charges. Phase three, which took place later that month, targeted the state's south-east and led to a host of further arrests and charges.

The sheer size of Operation Auxin put online child sex abuse into the Australian headlines. 'Up until that time, the broad view of Australian law enforcement, and probably Australians, was that this was something that happened in Europe,' Rouse says. It was not seen as 'an Australian problem'. Indeed, to this point, it was more likely that investigations into sex abuse would be prompted by a camera being handed over in a shop to have photographs developed. Content was being home-produced, but sporadically, and material being sent into Australia via the mail was often picked up – Customs staff would alert police, who would then make an arrest. 'But this was the dawn of the internet still,' Rouse says. Operation Auxin opened the nation's eyes to how big a problem child sex abuse might be, and the role of the internet in facilitating and even hiding it. The headlines were endless: more than 700 people targeted in a single investigation.

The identities of those arrested also drew political and public attention to the problem of child sex abuse. 'Raids expose huge child porn ring,' a headline screamed.[3] The crackdown had unveiled a complicated network involving people in positions of authority, then federal justice minister Chris Ellison told reporters.[4] Many of those apprehended held positions of trust in the community.

The sting nabbed police officers (including one who'd been assigned to investigate child abuse), teachers, a military officer, a minister of religion, nurses, doctors, truck drivers, a computer technician and insurance agent, an emergency services worker, a childcare centre owner and public servants. All up, more than 154 people across Australia – in every jurisdiction, with the exception of the Australian Capital Territory – stood charged with 2000 child sex offences, including rape. Ellison also revealed that the AFP had seized more than 380 computers. They discovered two million child pornography images depicting children aged between two and sixteen – one showed a two-year-old being subjected to bondage.[5] Police also found amateur home photographic studios and equipment used to produce child sex images.

'It gave everybody a sense of how many of these individuals live amongst us,' Rouse says. Up until then, investigations largely had centred on historical allegations, particularly relating to institutionalised abuse. But this was a different brand of abuse. It involved the here and now – today was perhaps more dangerous than yesterday. And many of the people caught up in the national sting were respectable, seemingly law-abiding Australian citizens. Some of them were the people who parents trusted to run the childcare centre that looked after their toddler, or the teacher who stood at the front of a class or leaned over a child to explain a difficult concept. Even the authors of public policy and police officers, who'd sworn to uphold the law, had been arrested. It seemed no industry was exempt. The raids changed the public narrative in Australia. 'They are judges. They are doctors. They are lawyers. They are police officers. They stack shelves at supermarkets. They teach. They do every possible job,' Rouse says. The fact that the number of arrests was so high and headlined news in almost every state and territory put sex abuse crime-fighting efforts in the spotlight. And they showed offenders were willing to sign up with their own personal credit card details to obtain access to websites containing child sex abuse.

The fallout from Operation Auxin, described by authorities as the largest national law enforcement operation in Australian history, was phenomenal. Six of those arrested later took their own lives. Families split. Communities tried to patch up heartache. In Victoria, government officials had to track down the parents of children attending certain childcare centres and explain that a senior administrator had been arrested. In Queensland, seven children were rescued after having been abused over a number of years; several of them had fallen victim to one paedophile who lived locally. Then detective inspector Brian Huxley told the media that the children ranged in age from five to thirteen and had been identified through images found on a seized computer. 'I don't think that these children would have been spared this abuse if it hadn't been for the fact that they were identified now,' Huxley said. 'I don't want to overdramatise it but really they have been rescued from further abuse.'[6] In each case, parents were unaware their children were victims.

The heartbreak didn't stop there. In Western Australia, a serving police officer and two teachers were amongst the twenty-one people arrested, with thirty-seven charges laid. Northern Territory police labelled the photographs seized there as the worst they had ever seen. In the Top End, seven men were arrested after raids on fourteen homes across Darwin, Alice Springs and Tennant Creek. Then NSW police commissioner Ken Moroney spoke for many when he told reporters: 'These are the most heinous, vile, despicable crimes against the child. As a commissioner of police, as a father and as a grandfather, I cannot think of a more vile crime in this community [than] the abuse of children, particularly the pornographic abuse of children.'[7] In Moroney's state, 100 000 child abuse images were seized, along with 2000 CDs, 300 videos and 200 computers. And on it went.

The fact that an estimated 40 per cent of the offenders were married men with children had consequences that rolled on and on. It was this statistic that led Natalie Walker to establish PartnerSPEAK, an organisation that supports the non-offending partners and children of those facing charges. Rouse said that, until Operation Auxin, he hadn't spent much time contemplating the enormous impact that an arrest could have on an alleged offender's family. Often, they were the breadwinner. Frequently, they held respected positions – on school councils or volunteer rosters, at church, in business groups, in sporting teams. Then, all of a sudden, they were plucked from their family, leaving partners and children to try to provide a narrative that made sense to close family, school communities, sporting teams, even strangers. 'They had no clue of who they had been living with,' Rouse says. And often, in his experience, the non-offending partner would allow the offending partner back into the family because they had no-one else or nowhere else to turn to.

Rouse says he learned a lot from Natalie Walker, the young woman behind PartnerSPEAK which provides support for those left behind, about what happened after police kicked in a door. 'She opened my eyes. We, the cops, riding on the white horse, arresting the offender and walking away. And we don't even think about the damage,' Rouse says. 'Can you imagine across 700 people [in Operation Auxin], married men, kids, families, aunts, uncles, brothers, all have had this person taken out of their lives now and we walk away and they're left to go, "What the hell?" I learned from this that we need to be very conscious of the non-offending partners in these circumstances. They're left going, "Somebody help me. What happened here? Where do I go? Who do I talk to?"' They, too, become victims when an abuser is caught.

In the United States, the president and technical administrator of the Belarus-based child pornography and money-laundering enterprise were each sentenced to twenty-five years in federal prison. One had been arrested at a Paris restaurant after he'd been persuaded to travel to France in a ruse set up by US federal agents; the other was holidaying in Spain when detained. They were just two of the dozens of court cases that followed the money trail around America and several other countries. But these two bigwigs in a commercial venture prompted those chasing online sex abuse to reflect on how they needed to police this abhorrent crime going forward. US district judge Dennis M Cavanaugh said that after Regpay's principals' prison terms expired, they would be required to serve another five years on supervised release.[8] US attorney Christopher J Christie didn't mince his words on their conviction: 'Child pornography and those who profit from it are a blight on civilised society. These two defendants will spend their adult lives in prison because they care more about money than the lives of innocent young children.'[9]

Australia's crime fighters were much praised over Operation Auxin, for revealing a nasty new underbelly of crime, where websites played host to child abuse, and people from all walks of life signed up for it. It signalled to Rouse and his team that they needed to continually adapt their policing to stay ahead of the predators. Sex abusers had found a new way to exploit children, and law enforcement needed to disrupt their own practices to stay relevant. Taskforce Argos had its roots in sex abuse that had been waged against children in institutions, mostly by those whose job it was to care for them – churches and orphanages stood out as stamping grounds for some paedophiles. But technological change now allowed child abuse images to be quickly captured and shared, and online distribution promised bigger markets and greater volumes of exploitative material. The operation also rammed home how the internet could host this awful maltreatment, and draw in like-minded criminals to share their caches of abuse. Operation Auxin was full of lessons.

Jon Rouse had decided years earlier that, increasingly, the challenge facing his team in fighting child abuse would be the future, not the past. Now, his team was learning the size and breadth of that challenge.

6

Partners against crime

It was over a quick lunch, inside a Gold Coast mall, that the seeds were sown to investigate online child sex rackets in a different way. It was codenamed Operation Achilles, and history will label it the probe that built a concrete international commitment to hunt down child sex offenders. But it did much more than that. It prompted the use of laws usually reserved for organised crime in the United States. It gave birth to more than a hundred other investigations around the world. It initiated an historic agreement on the deployment of undercover officers between the FBI and Taskforce Argos. It revealed, in alarming detail, how dark web predators learned to build structures, akin to companies, to protect both their identities and their sordid secrets. Operation Achilles, which gathered 400 000 pieces of evidence in twenty-six months, also pitted predators against police in what played out like a game of chess.

Operation Achilles began in January 2006 after New Zealand authorities arrested a man who then sought a plea bargain in return for information on the secret online child sex club of which he was a member. That information was passed onto Argos because of possible Australian connections, and with the man's passwords, Argos became a covert 'member' of 'the Group'. Several months later, then Queensland police commissioner Bob Atkinson told Jon Rouse that he wanted him to meet an FBI agent who was speaking on the Gold Coast. His name was Arnold Bell, and he was the new head of the FBI's innocent images taskforce, after a career spent fighting gangs, bank robbers and organised crime on the streets of Los Angeles. Bell was travelling to Australia to detail how he wanted to take his FBI unit down the path of tackling more serious crime – and he'd be Down Under for exactly eight hours.

Rouse and Peter Crawford, also from Taskforce Argos, sat in the audience for Bell's presentation and grabbed him for a coffee immediately afterwards. 'We just clicked,' Rouse says. 'He was in and out of Australia so we went shopping in the mall so he could get some gifts and have a quick lunch.' That brief moment in time laid the foundation for years of teamwork that continues today. Arnold Bell says Rouse and Crawford told him about the investigation of the New Zealand links they had started, which had tentacles in the United States. That prompted non-committal chatter about the value of having covert operatives in each other's countries. Not long after, they met again in Washington, DC and sealed a deal for an FBI special agent to be embedded with Taskforce Argos on Operation Achilles in Australia.

Bell, who is now retired after serving twenty-five years in the FBI, many of them spent in very senior positions, says the special agent reported back to him within a couple of weeks: 'He said, "Hey, this is a really big deal." Some of the targets they identified and monitored were people that we were looking at [in the United States], but we had no idea who they were. We knew they were players in that space.'

It wasn't long before Brenden Power, an Australian police officer, boarded a plane to go and work for eighteen months as a covert operative for the FBI in America. Power had failed to make the cut as a police officer in New South Wales, but Queensland had been looking for cleanskins in the wake of the Commission of Inquiry into Possible Illegal Activities and Associated Police Misconduct, also known as the Fitzgerald Inquiry, which tore apart the government and found shocking examples of corruption in the police service. Power graduated in 1990, the year after Fitzgerald reported, and moved to Taskforce Argos fifteen years later. Power, who had never left Australia's shores, told his family he'd be away for some time to join an investigation into paedophiles, and with his first ever passport, he boarded a plane for Maryland. His new home was across the road from a covert FBI building: on one side of his living quarters were a couple whose domestic arguments kept him up at night, while on the other side were fairly constant drug-fuelled parties.

International collaboration was already part of policing in this area of crime, as evidenced by New Zealand authorities contacting Taskforce Argos. But embedding agents in another nation's covert operations? That was a recognition that child sex crimes would never, ever respect borders, and that it would take a new type of policing to combat it. And it was the first time, anywhere in the world, that a protracted infiltration of a child sex offender network would occur. Bell gives kudos to his boss at the FBI, Steve

Tidwell, and to Bob Atkinson, who he nominates as one of the globe's great police leaders, for cultivating the liaison which created a template for crime cooperation. 'We're all on the same team,' Bell says, adding that fights over individual roles and territories should always fall away 'when you're trying to save kids'.

Mike Duffey knows this all too well. Duffey supervises the Florida Department of Law Enforcement's cyber high-tech crime unit, which conducts online child probes. More than 120 staff report to him, and his unit covers twenty-two million people. He remembers being a uniformed officer, working narcotic cases. 'And it was very territorial. It was, "This is my case, these are my informants,"' he says. Saving kids is different – he has woken up Rouse in the middle of the night with a tip, and vice versa. Ignoring boundaries is important because online child sex crimes often are real-time offences that require the involvement of several agencies in several countries. 'You're protecting a child versus going after a drug dealer who's part of a criminal organisation,' he says.

•

The security around joining and remaining a member of the Group was impregnable, a detail that was explained to the Queensland Organised Crime Commission of Inquiry in 2015. The Group had been operating for fifteen years before police became aware of it, and its growth had been protected by security measures such as the encryption of operating systems, firewalls, port scanning, proxies and anonymising services which meant the IP could not be tracked. 'The administrators also developed software that allowed movie files to be split into segments, with the order of the segments being altered,' the inquiry reported. 'This resulted in the movie file being unable to be played unless a member employed the de-encryption process required.'[1] These measures were the brainchild of the Group's leader, who used the moniker Canary and told members that 'a true pedo will know all files in their collection, and will remember enough about each image to be able to answer specific questions'. Applicants also needed to have an extensive image library. Steve Tidwell, the FBI executive assistant director who oversaw the bureau's national crime programs at the time, later explained that the site's administrators 'went to a lot of trouble to keep from being discovered ... They had a level of operational security that we've not seen before.'[2]

The Group's leadership required fresh and regular abuse to be uploaded by members to add to an already extensive image library, and to retain membership. 'They were like stamp collectors,' Rouse says. Those wanting to sign up were tested on recognising images in their own collections. 'The group administrators developed a software application that was sent to the prospective member, which allowed an analysis of the person's hard file and image contents,' the organised crime commission explained. 'The prospective member was then asked for specific details of images in the collection.'[3] This was aimed at outwitting law enforcement, but it also allowed site administrators to view the extent of the image collection held by a prospective member.

It was this level of security that signalled to Argos the battle it faced in dismantling the Group, as well as the seriousness of the abuse being waged against children. So, with the New Zealand offender wanting to make a plea bargain, Argos decided to hunker down and find out what it could before any comfort was provided to the man sitting in a Kiwi jail cell. And that was the start of Operation Achilles, named for the goal of finding the Group's weak spot.

The reach of this international dark web child sex racket stood out. Its users were known to live across the globe, because of tiny hints they dropped and which were picked up by Achilles' covert operative Brenden Power. The Group's leader was evangelical in his posts, advocating for a community where it was acceptable to have sex with children. 'Imagine a time when a picture is just a picture,' Canary tells his secret flock in one intercepted message. 'And those who view them are not vilified. Follow me to a museum where dreams come true.' In the accompanying movie, he takes members on a tour of his Louvre, where the pictures all show graphic child exploitation. As Argos dug deeper, it found unprecedented exploitation. 'Mala is to die for in those pigtails,' one message read. 'I have a few 5yo [year old] Millies that you do not have,' another user offered. 'Just dropping in for a hot minute ... to help out the dry spell, and to give everyone something to do for an afternoon,' said another. The cases of two girls whose images frequently circulated within the Group – Monica and Marietta, whose story is told in Chapter 7 – prompted a new investigation based in Belgium. Their inclusion in movies and images showed that members of the Group had the opportunity to 'order' the rape of a child, and to even direct how it might occur. This was rape on demand, Rouse says. Paying members could order a particular camera angle and the type of sex to be had with a particular child – not just Monica and Marietta, but others too. Even their age and what they wore could be chosen, until their clothes were removed in an assault which would colour their lives.

With the Group's users residing in a number of countries, law enforcement banded together in a way that was prodigious. Operation Achilles spanned five nations, three continents and eleven American states. At its close, Arnold Bell said Achilles had 'pulled some of the most heinous actors off the street who would still be abusing right now, but for this investigation'. Spin-off cases ran into the hundreds, he says, each of those leading to more arrests, and rescues. 'So when you arrest these guys around the world,' says Bell, 'you get their digital evidence and you start exporting that evidence; you start to find all their connections.' He adds that Achilles recorded the 'largest digital seizure in the history of the FBI at the time'. Hard drives were found buried in all sorts of places, including deep underground in backyards. All up, fifty-eight terabytes of material was collected.

With a career that has filled his home with awards, Bell remembers Achilles for the teamwork that spanned the law enforcement world. He says that was highlighted on one occasion when search and arrest warrants were simultaneously actioned around the world, for the first time. He remembers being in the FBI command centre in Washington, DC: 'The Germans were calling in. The Canadians were calling in. And of course, the Australians were calling in – and they were all hitting houses at the same time, which was pretty cool.' Bell says thirty-two children were rescued in the United States by the time he left the operation, and another 'forty or so' rescues came after. Rouse says an investigation sometimes has to end because of the risks of keeping it going – people have been identified, and they talk. That often drove the timing of the global 'takedown'. Rouse was at home in suburban Brisbane as the raids rippled around the world, with some, where law enforcement were aware of other factors, involving snipers and special weapons teams. Rouse says that while the arrests signalled the extent of the dark web clubs, this was secondary to the number of children saved. That was at the heart of investigators' work. He repeats one of his core convictions: 'Arrests are not a significant part of my life. Child rescues are my performance indicator.'

Monica and Marietta were plucked to safety in a side investigation in Belgium tagged Operation Koala because the leads came from Australia. Arabella Suzette and Yvette Daisy were another two young girls unearthed by Taskforce Argos's covert operative. They featured in a movie available to members deep inside the Group, in which an adult male has two girls, aged around five and three, sitting next to him. What follows is horrendous to see, with the children ordered to perform various sexual tasks. And as they do, the offender talks to them. It was clear to Taskforce Argos that German was the language being spoken. Then, in a slip-up that perhaps had the crime fighters high-fiving each other, because it was a vital clue, the man used the girls' names. Another voice can be heard, too, indicating they are being filmed, with a producer also giving instructions in the background. Music is audible as well. Argos officers packaged it up and sent it to police in Germany.

Detective Chief Inspector Daniel Szumilas was a case officer with German police when the information came through from Australia. He had previously met Rouse at the Interpol meeting in France where Steve Irwin had introduced the Australian investigator. He was drawn to investigating crimes against children, he says, because of two ever-present factors: 'The child is always innocent. And secondly, they are always defenceless and vulnerable. That's what makes this work so special for me. That's what motivates me.' So does the level of intelligence swapping between countries, which Szumilas says has saved countless lives. He highlights this point by detailing a case involving a video portraying the severe abuse of several boys. The limited language on the video – a short whisper – was not German. The video was uploaded into a virtual working space that was used as part of a multi-country team effort, with the investigators' focus turning to a low-resolution image of a ticket with illegible writing. 'And officers from Spain immediately said, "That's a metro ticket from Madrid," because if you live in Madrid, and use the metro regularly, you immediately recognise it,' he says. Soon after, the case was solved and several boys were rescued.

Szumilas, who has been a police officer for almost thirty years since leaving school aged nineteen, also remembers the case of Arabella Suzette and Yvette Daisy. It was similar to the Spanish metro case, he says, with arrests and children saved within days. Szumilas arrived at work early one morning to find a request from Rouse, to which was attached dreadful footage of prepubescent girls being sexually abused by a man who spoke in a German accent and called the girls by two specific – and unusual – names.

Szumilas jotted down the names and conducted an open Google search. Within a minute, two sisters popped up with those names, and then a family website which provided an address. Thirty minutes later, Szumilas had a positive identification. The address was then searched, the perpetrator arrested – and later jailed for ten years – and the children saved. 'I feel a little bit embarrassed because it was so easy,' Szumilas says, but he acknowledges this was only because of the unprecedented international cooperation around Operation Achilles. 'We didn't know about these videos and who knows when we would have found them,' he says. Taskforce Argos found them, and Szumilas, himself the father of two girls, found the victims.

Operation Achilles is full of successes like this. Paul Griffiths remembers looking at the UK end of the Group, where many members didn't produce their own material but were experts at sourcing previously unseen abuse. One predator uploaded images and footage investigators had never seen but which was clearly from the United Kingdom. The detail on a cardboard removal box provided Griffiths with a rough location of where the victim might be, but it was a recliner chair that provided the key clues. Griffiths identified it and then, using delivery records, tracked its journey to an address. 'We had a video of her being raped when she was seven,' Griffiths says. By the time her molester was identified, she had been abused for at least six years, and at thirteen was living with him.

'Sometimes it is being in the right place at the right time,' Rouse says. 'Or being in there for so long that you pick up a mistake. Often it's just bloody brilliant detective work by some of our people.' Here, he's talking about both covert operators and victim identification specialists, like Paul Griffiths and Warren Bulmer, whose work is recognised globally. One tiny step leads to another, and another, and another. Like many other investigators, Rouse remembers something of each case. In regard to the girl rescued in the United Kingdom as a result of Griffiths' work, it was her voice – Rouse had heard her pleading with her attacker to leave her alone. She was one of the children who were rescued. In some of those cases, law enforcement crews crept into a home and nabbed a child; in others, they knocked down the front door in a bid to surprise the perpetrator and save the child at a moment's notice. The method is fit for purpose, with the goal to take children away from a world of torment many have known for as long as they can remember.

But on some days, Rouse continues to wear like a cloak the heartbreak of not finding victims. There's another girl, called Girl 1, but let's give her the name Millie, and Achilles investigators watched her grow up, being abused. Brenden Power says investigators kept getting so close, with Bulmer zeroing in on the crime scene by focusing on tiny, tiny clues, but for a long time, none of their work located her. He says he looked at thousands of images and hundreds of videos, but he only had to find them and refer them on. It was Bulmer and Griffiths who had to sit and watch them over and over again, to pull out small details in the hope they were the clues that would lead them to Millie. They did that for 'three or four years'.

Arnold Bell pauses before he answers questions about Millie. You can fight gangs on the streets of Los Angeles and still struggle with the memory of a young girl who deserved so much more. 'You are watching this young lady grow up in this abusive situation,' he says. Silence again before he says: 'That is horrific.' But Millie appeared to be too well hidden and investigators just couldn't find her (Millie's story is told in Chapter 8).

Another child popped up just as Operation Achilles was winding down. A new member joined the secret club, and this child featured in his uploads. Her face was never visible, nor her feet, just a torso signalling a very young child, perhaps even a baby. The abuser shared details no-one should ever hear – ever. He was even warned by other members of the Group not to provide any clues for investigators to track down, and to ensure all images of the child were safeguarded by removing any metadata – information that potentially signals when and where images were taken – before posting them. Investigators raced to find this child. 'We had nothing,' Rouse says. When I ask him what happened to her, Rouse's silence delivers the answer. 'If the operation had gone longer, we might have had more time to engage with him,' he says. 'He might have posted more images. He might have made a mistake. But we didn't have time because we were in the final tactical phase of the operation. Briefings had already occurred.' Rouse comes back to this unknown child much later, after our discussion has moved on. 'She was probably two or three,' he says. 'You don't forget those children.'

Warren Bulmer remembers the case of this little girl as if it was yesterday. He managed to track down the serial number on the camera used in the assaults, and wrote to the camera's manufacturer with pressing questions: When was it sold? Where? To whom? 'And they wouldn't cooperate.' Bulmer almost spits out the last sentence. He's thinking of a child, but a corporation is choosing to hide behind some law so as to not provide the information that might save her.

As I travel through this project, the overwhelming role that hope plays for each investigator becomes clear. I ask Bulmer if this tiny child was ever saved? 'She might have been,' he says. Or alternatively, as an adult, she might have revealed the sexual assault and embarked on therapy. Hope. Bell says officers learn the hard way about the importance of moving on. Investigations had to have an end point because of finite resources and competing priorities, but also because of the need to time the arrests and rescues for maximum impact. 'I take comfort in the fact that we saved a bunch of kids,' Bell says. 'I can dwell on what we didn't get, but there's no point. What's the use of that?'

•

Operation Achilles ran for two years, until February 2008. Arrests were made across the United States, United Kingdom, Germany and Australia. In Townsville, a senior member of the Group was later sentenced to jail for six years. A Victorian man was also jailed. Globally, more than sixty children were rescued, twenty-two network members were arrested, and four commercial child exploitation websites were dismantled. It was the most sophisticated child abuse ring the FBI had ever seen. The response was a determination by crime fighters, everywhere, to match this new sophistication with new ways of tracking down and punishing offenders. For example, in the United States, it prompted the inaugural use of a federal statute that had been signed by US president George Bush a couple of years earlier. The *Adam Walsh Child Protection and Safety Act* arranged sex offenders into three tiers, depending on the severity of the crime. The most serious offenders were required to update their whereabouts every three months on release from any jail term, for life.

This ring had been run like a business, with specific roles for different members, and with orders coming from the top. Perverted and cruel images served as their currency. Brenden Power, who spent eighteen months inside the Group in the United States, deserves credit for much of the groundwork, which heralded a new era of cooperation: the exchange of coverts, timed operations, and an information swap between Germany, the United Kingdom, the United States, Canada and Australia.

The operation also threw up a new type of child sex abuser: an entrepreneur who knew what they were up against. 'I think it is very unwise to assume that law enforcement is not capable of evolving a strategy designed to work where their previous ones have patently failed,' the Group's leader, Canary, told its members. 'Given their law enforcement way of thinking, we're probably one of the best organised child porn rings on the Usenet.' But it wasn't safe, said Canary, 'to assume that law enforcement agencies know nothing about us or that they're not seeking us, and we're responsible for our own security'. He then floated an idea: they would change their names and encryption details and adopt themes ranging from cooking to cars, just in case investigators were on their tail. And all the while, Brenden Power was listening in and gathering evidence.

Power says he saw being a covert as more of a 'technical challenge' than anything else. He says he would have struggled to play the character of a paedophile. 'I wasn't good at being able to write the way they write and speak the way they speak,' he says. But their communication was largely by text on online bulletin boards, and the shorter the message, the better. Power says his value was in understanding the Group's encryption methods, how they transferred information, and being able to 'decrypt and then re-encode' data. Certainly the conversations were 'off-putting' and the material 'horrendous', but the volume meant he raced from one image to another. It was the job of others to dissect them. 'If it was a movie sequence, I'd watch the first couple of seconds,' he says. That was it. Then he'd pass it on to victim identification experts or the relevant country's law enforcement teams. He also had to be deft at scanning different parts of the Group despite the strong security.

Operation Achilles bubbled with learnings that have been the basis of investigations since. For one thing, it provided insights into the minds of those who rule these ugly underworld clubs that continue to grow in popularity. But while Canary's dark web comments have been studied by FBI profilers, he's never been found. Investigators believe he had military-level intelligence and could have been a high-ranking government employee. 'The chessboard is a world,' Canary told members at one point. 'The pieces are the law and the Group. The rules of the game are encoded into the justice system. The player on the other side is hidden from us. We know that his play is always patient, and we know, to our cost, that he never overlooks a mistake, or makes the smallest allowance for ignorance.' He was equating the cat-and-mouse game with investigators with a game of chess. Rouse says: 'This is the absolute leader of the Group. We know that he was in the US.' And he showed how depraved he was by guiding club members in the viewing of a horrible movie where he glued together sixteen or so segments of a video depicting an infant being raped, and then put a heavy metal soundtrack under it. Only those who had the encryption kit could see it. 'That was what he felt the Group was all about,' Rouse says.

This was Canary's message to those viewing that movie, which was tagged Baby Kia:

We are united although invisible, like the choir in the background. There is a door with no visible window, no hinges, no handle, no obvious way to get in. My symbol is on the door, although the actual mechanics are not obvious and there is no way to know who is really operating the door, or even if there is more than one person involved. As one approaches things become clearer. Although the apprehension and mystery remain. One can only come so close and the process of scanning begins. When finished, I blend back into the background and the show begins.

The chess analogy fired up investigators, including Rouse. But it's a telling one. On one side of the board sit the pieces owned by the law enforcement community: intelligence, covert operatives, planning, strategy, hard work and passion. 'On our side we've also got foreign law enforcement agency partners,' Rouse says. They are all arrayed against, on the other side, an army of security figures: operational security, membership vetting, and the anonymity offered on the dark web. Sometimes, legislation, policy and resource limitations help the strategy of the baddies. 'And they can do whatever they bloody like,' Rouse says. 'There are no rules for them except the ones that they write for themselves, which are how you will talk, how you will engage, how you use encryption – all of the things that are set up to protect themselves.'

Investigators learned that Canary had a couple of deputies, including a male called 'Helen' in the United Kingdom, and he carefully covered both his tracks and his identity. But they knew he made all the important chess moves. He set the rules, monitored the club's security, and encouraged pay-for-production videos, which equated to rape on demand. Taking down Canary was crucial to dismantling his network and saving those being assaulted within it. But communications inside the Group ran into hundreds of thousands of messages, and Taskforce Argos and the FBI had to track each one in the hope that a single careless mistake would lead them to Canary's identity and location. Rouse says mistakes were made, but he will not be drawn on them because similar clubs, with hundreds of thousands of members, are on the dark web today, plying their sick trade, and he doesn't want to signal investigators' next move. Patience here genuinely is the winning virtue. Rouse will only say that a simple mistake on the part of a user can lead to a computer IP address, which then provides more clues, and that's how offenders started to be identified in various countries. 'A lot of these child sex offender groups put themselves up there as just being untouchable,' Rouse says. 'It really is like a game of chess, perhaps. And it's nice to tip the queen over. Or even the king.'

At one stage in Operation Achilles, the investigators thought they actually had a checkmate. They located a lake and camping grounds in the United States and combed through car records, all of it hinting at a trail that would lead them to the Group's leader. Alas, it proved a dead end, although Jon Rouse doesn't believe that means investigators were defeated in Canary's chess game: 'He lost his entire board. So I would suggest that what happened was that he just continued moving around and moving around ... So let's just call it a draw.'

And yet Rouse knows he's not speaking convincingly here, for a simple reason. While dozens of children were saved, including Monica and Marietta, and Arabella and Yvette, Operation Achilles ended without investigators finding Girl 1 – Millie – who they saw being abused year after year after year, nor the other, tiny child who only appeared on the eve of Achilles' closure and whose head and feet were always hidden.

Part 3

On the case

7

Finding Monica and Marietta

It's just one sentence, but covert operative Brenden Power knows what it means the moment he's intercepted it. 'Okay folks, the one you've all been waiting for – the Monica extra-special video,' the online author writes. The video was made by special request, and the organisers had paid US$120 towards its cost. 'That's quite a bargain on a per person basis,' continues the author. 'I won't spoil you with the details. Just download and watch it; making sure you have at least an hour of free time.'

Power, who at this point is still in Brisbane, yet to board a plane to join the FBI in Maryland, knows the heartache those words spell out, and he pops his head into his boss's office the moment Jon Rouse arrives at work. It's early in the morning of 12 July 2006. The city is still asleep, the sun at least an hour away from creeping over the horizon, but for Taskforce Argos and Jon Rouse, this is a golden hour: on the other side of the globe, in the United States and across Europe, investigators are at their desks and so it's easier to talk, to nut out strategies, to work out the next move. 'What do you want to do about this?' Power asks.

Together, they play the video. It never gets easier, but former police commissioner Bob Atkinson comments on Rouse's ability to 'compartmentalise', a knack he's seen in leaders across his forty-year career. 'They can look at this or that and then put it in a box, and walk away from it and go to the next case,' he says. Rouse and his peers look at the image or footage, but they also look beyond it to the metadata that might hold a secret, or even a product that appears somewhere within the four corners of the screen. Rarely in these images does an offender show his face. More often than not it will be a penis, or part of an arm or a hand that might hold a clue. The investigators look for a standout freckle or a mole, something that marks the offender, for later, when an arrest is near.

Audio, however, is particularly difficult to cope with. Rouse admits that: 'You hear children. That's a progression from an image where you are imagining what's going on, to hearing what's going on. You actually hear the children and the pain they're in.' Rouse also says, in many cases, audio can denote a deeper level of depravity, and those officers charged with identifying victims in footage will frequently work with the audio turned off. You only need to hear something that disturbing once.

In the video that Power and Rouse watch, it's the techno music that stands out. There are two children, who are talking. And there's a man, large on-screen, having sex with them. Yet despite the depravity, the children don't sound distraught. Perhaps they've done this dozens or even hundreds of times. They seem to know what to do, even though Rouse and Power suspect they are pre-teen. 'Maybe nine and twelve,' Rouse says. The video is a piece of evidence, perhaps like that first key jigsaw piece that offers a gigantic clue to the next part of the puzzle – and in this case leads to finding and saving two victims.

The investigators now turn to the commentary of those who have watched the video. That's where they hope to find other clues, such as IP addresses to track down, or language idiosyncrasies that might point to a particular continent or region. 'Holy cow,' one member says. 'I think I'm dreaming and I will realise it isn't true when I wake up. I always thought the YVM girls were from Russia, or from some other former Soviet Union Republic.' He goes on to say that, after hearing 'Monica' talk, she is obviously 'Dutch or Flemish'. He finishes with: 'Thank you very much for the video.'

Rouse and Power both have the same response: thank you very much for the clue. The next step is easier. The YVM – Young Video Models – website is downloaded, decoded, saved and archived. That will be evidence for later. But for now, the focus comes back to the two young girls in the video. Running down those who make the videos is crucial – every sex offender, and those who see value in capturing their crimes, need to be stopped, and there are millions of them worldwide, from all walks of life. But rescuing the children at the centre of the debauchery is always the primary goal of every investigation. This is difficult because online sex abuse rarely points directly to where the victims are, geographically. Daily, eyewitnesses help deliver indictments in crimes occurring within our communities, from break-ins to hit-and-runs to assaults.

But what about when the crimes occur behind a locked bedroom door, or in a cold hotel room with no pictures on the wall, and it's not even clear what country they are taking place in? Every detail counts – no clue can be missed.

Fortunately, this time Taskforce Argos has been given a massive lead. The website of young models includes two children whose names are Monica and Marietta. Immediately, Power and Rouse know they are the two little girls whose innocence is being stolen in the video footage being distributed across the world. But on this website they're in modelling gear. They're scantily dressed, like all the other models, but there's nothing to suggest the horrors being performed on another stage, and which are now in the hands of Taskforce Argos.

A money trail will help here, too. Rouse knows that viewers are accessing the Monica video, and most likely many others, by using their credit cards. 'This is commercially produced child exploitation material,' Rouse says. 'That's what we are thinking – and that we have a criminal enterprise going on here.' The Monica video pops up as part of Operation Achilles, the umbrella investigation that produces leads pointing to child abuse networks in the United States, Britain, France, Spain and Sweden, but it demands its own focus. In black and white, in the messages between members of this murky group whose numbers keep swelling, there's proof that this video has been funded. The details of this spilling out in chatter worries some members, and points to how those who trawl the dark web think. One member conveys his worry over what will happen if the authorities ever find Monica. 'They will follow the money trail and will go after the paying customers,' he says.

But he also admits to concern for Monica. His rationale is preposterous: he worries that Monica's future could be derailed, that she could be ripped away from the life she knows and become institutionalised. 'They don't think like we do,' Rouse says quietly.

If more proof of that is needed, it comes in this comment from another member: 'Sentiments aside, here's what I'd like to see in the next video.' Rouse won't admit it, but often when he talks about these cases, his eyes become sad. He's learned that this member, and thousands of others, might go to work today like almost everyone else. He could be married or single, have children or grandchildren, work on a building site or in a courtroom. On this occasion, from his language, the offender gives away very little – he's just another generic criminal, encouraging and applauding the abuse of two young girls. But what makes the hairs on the back of Rouse's neck stand up is what he hears next. Another member suggests where a monitor should be placed, and how one of the children should be positioned. He says this will assist Monica to play her role in another tawdry homemade movie.

Rouse leaves his office almost immediately. He knows the assistant commissioner of state crime operations, Peter Swindells, will understand what he's about to say: 'I'm seriously concerned about Monica and Marietta. We need to find them. This group is going to keep funding videos if we don't do something about the over-arching crime syndicate.' Rouse is wondering what request might be made by a member of this dark web group next. 'What we were seeing was children being raped on demand at the instruction of a child sex offender network that we were in,' says Rouse. He told Swindells that unless urgent action was taken, further requests by the offenders would happen – and they had to try and stop it.

Rouse sees the best response as working with the FBI. The relationship between Argos and the FBI has been growing stronger, nurtured by the Queensland Police hierarchy and investigators tracking down leads that don't stop at borders. 'But this was a precedent,' Rouse says. And a game changer. 'What we were seeing we had to stop. We couldn't let that happen to a kid.' Swindells acquiesces immediately, and soon, Brenden Power sets off for America to tap into the dark clubs that hide online child sex abuse, a post he will hold for eighteen months. Rouse, at home in Australia, turns his attention back to Monica, and the child exploitation website that has members fanned out across Europe.

•

Taskforce Argos sets up a virtual workplace where Rouse uploads everything relevant to Monica and Marietta: every single communication from the network, every video, every clue that might give their colleagues in Europe a fighting chance to find the girls. 'In my head, we have to follow the money,' Rouse says. 'We need to find her. And if we can find her, we can find the offender. We can find the photographer. We can find the webmaster. And then we can find the financials. That's what was running through my head.' Anders Persson, whom Rouse had befriended during a presentation to an Interpol specialist group, is on board immediately, gathering together a group of international experts from Germany, the Netherlands and Belgium. 'I've just dropped the text postings from the news group for you to read,' Rouse writes to Persson. 'Of course, the safety of this child is paramount. And if she's in your jurisdiction, then finding her and arresting the offender is a priority.' He also tells Persson that at least one of the children is definitely from Holland, a clue gleaned from the indiscreet chatter of one of the Group's members. But, he adds, light, quick steps are necessary, to manage the media. Those members will be alerted to the end of any movie production, and investigators need to nab as many of them as they can. This joint effort is called Operation Koala because of its Australian origins.

Dutch officer Eric Kuijl is quickly in touch. He has received a message from a police peer in Belgium who listened to the videos and determined that the language spoken was Dutch as used in the Flanders region in the country's north. One word provided the missing piece of the puzzle. Either Monica or Marietta had said *stoel*, the Dutch word for 'chair'. That directs investigators to a particular region of Belgium near the North Sea coast. Back in Brisbane, Rouse receives another lead. Intelligence from talk amongst members of the child abuse ring suggests Monica previously came to the attention of police over her model photographs. 'Perhaps, there may be some case file on the child that may help ... just a thought,' says Rouse of his thinking at the time. Brenden Power, meanwhile, now deep inside both the FBI and this dark club, decrypts the conversation of a member talking about Monica being sexually assaulted.

That discussion of the assault sets a lit match to a forest of tired old wood. It outrages members of the closed group inside their dark web haven, not because of the attack itself, the violation of Monica, but because of the violation of their treasured internal security. Members lash out at each other. Through this post, this malicious talk of a child being assaulted, someone has betrayed others' trust. The falling-out has repercussions. Through the angry exchanges, investigators learn that what is being promoted is just a short clip of a bigger video. Greed has prompted one member to make mini videos and trade them for other content on other forums. Don't worry, members are told, 'Sergio' has already found the person responsible.

Sergio. Six letters. Investigators are ecstatic. A name. And judging by the conversation, it is someone high up the ranks of this criminal enterprise, a decision-maker. The hubris of the group's leadership then provides a bread trail for Power, Rouse, Kuijl, Persson and the other investigators working across borders to find the two young girls. Someone who is part of the group's leadership boasts that their operation is probably 'just too big' for police to handle. They go on: 'Also 99.9% of the stuff that's posted is old, so they have to sift through 1000s of posts to find anything new, which is surely what they will be mainly interested in. We know that Monica was investigated once but why? Because she talked too much at school. It wasn't through investigation of the Young Video Models website. I suspect that even when they investigate [sic] her they didn't actually see the film she made at that point in time.'

The arrogance of the members is unbelievable. But it doesn't match the determination of the investigators hell-bent on bringing them down. Rouse is more humble than proud, but in a scrap online, you'd have him at unbackable odds.

Another post comes in, in which a senior member of the group gloats that the law enforcement record for stopping the distribution of child exploitation material is 'pitiful'. And then this: 'Let's just hope and pray that I'm right for Monica's sake.' Rouse smiles at the memory of this revelation. It's not something you see often, but this tracking down of sex offenders is the race of his life. He's spent decades doing it, from 4 a.m. until the sun goes down at night. In Operation Koala, he rarely offered information; each fact had to be 'extracted', always headlined by an explanation that this was teamwork. And so it proved to be. A few hours after that post, Dutch authorities landed at the door of the man who was abusing the girls on camera. The 'film set' where he raped the two young girls was discovered in a nondescript bedroom at an inn in the city of Bruges.

Rouse, as Bob Atkinson pointed out, has a rare ability to file horror in different compartments inside his head. He's learned how to do it over time, and to turn off: by playing in his rock band, or walking along a beach without talking to anyone. This time – he's not sure why – it was different. A few years later, while delivering training to Belgium investigators, he was drawn to Bruges, to the inn where this horror was filmed. He had a single day off on that trip, and on it, he caught a train to where Monica's and Marietta's innocence was stolen. 'I found the Bauhaus and I just sat there,' he says. 'Just sat. It was a closure thing.'

•

The arrest of the offender led investigators up the chain of command to Sergio Marzola, who was believed to have made 150 videos in Ukraine, the Netherlands and Belgium. He was apprehended in Bologna, in northern Italy, a day before he was due to move to Ukraine, where prosecutors determined he ran a studio for producing many of the abuse films. But the net was spread wider than that. The man in the videos, investigators discovered, was paid to showcase horrible sex abuse; many others were, too. By the close of Operation Koala, eighteen separate European police forces had fingered almost 1000 child sex offenders, arrested 180 'high-profile' offenders and identified forty victims. The ripple effect fuelled operations in other countries. The FBI says one conducted in the United States, spurred by the 50 000 emails picked up during Operation Koala, led to the rescue of fourteen girls, some as young as three years old; the arrest of 170 adults; and the dismantling of seven major child pornography rings.

'The internet has connected all of us into one world without oceans and boundaries,' observes Shawn Henry, one-time FBI Cyber Division assistant director.[1] This goes to Rouse's point that work done in downtown Brisbane or in a tiny office in Belgium or through the FBI in Washington can have a real impact on children everywhere. 'We have always thought outside the borders,' he says, 'and I've been challenged multiple times in my career about whether this is work on behalf of the people of Queensland. I don't care where the kid is. I don't know where the child or the offender is until I know where the child or the offender is. They could be in Queensland. So I've got to do the work to find them. And when I find them, and they're in the US or in the UK or somewhere [else] in Europe, that doesn't mean I don't do something.' This is a contentious point amongst some crime-fighting bodies, because it is taxpayers' money in particular states or countries that fund local investigators. But Rouse's argument answers that: until a child is found, investigators don't know in what country she or he might be, and that's why investigators argue that every child in every image needs to be found.

Marzola, a then 42-year-old Italian national, was found to be the sole producer of the business filming Monica and Marietta, and also up to thirty other businesses, which authorities said had generated considerable profits. Indeed, when Marzola was found, the Italian media reported he had €150000 in cash hidden in stereo speakers.[2] He was sentenced to ten years' jail. Marzola charged different amounts of money for children to be filmed in specific clothing, naked or while being raped, and then sold those images and footage through bulletin boards that were encrypted, with passwords – and payment – required to access them. Investigators found that individuals would pay hundreds of euros for their preferred model to pose in a particular way. They were able to order the young children to stand or sit or lie, or to send lingerie for the children to wear. Some even paid extra to be present at the film shoots, while others paid for the children, some still young enough to go to primary school, to hold a piece of paper bearing the user's name, as a depraved memento. Exploitation on demand. Rouse shakes his head as he revisits the horror in his mind.

In some countries in 2006, internet speed didn't allow for downloads, but those customers didn't miss out. Instead, they were required to send cash, and in exchange, DVDs were mailed to their address. By today's standards, it was low-tech, but money bought more than a movie in many instances. In total, child abuse videos had been produced and sold to 2500 customers – including lawyers, school teachers, students and unemployed individuals – in nineteen countries. Nine men were arrested and charged for buying the videos in Australia, and a four-year-old girl who was being abused – although not as part of the video production – was rescued. The footage of Monica and Marietta was part of a library that showed off girls aged nine to sixteen. Aside from Monica and Marietta, all twenty-three victims were found to be from Ukraine, but each of them had their own story. Rouse rattles off their names, which are seared into his mind. Helena, born on 23 October 1991. Her videos were titled 'H'. She was the sister of Alex. Mariana was accompanied by her grandmother and older sister to the 'fashion shoots'. Her videos were titled 'M'. Khristina was accompanied by her mother, Leena, too.

Rouse still has a folder of unsolved cases that he's marked 'weeds', so named because sometimes that which is unwanted grows at a remarkable speed. The environment helps determine that. One operation doesn't bring a strategic impact on the commercial exploitation of children. 'You've got impoverished families across Europe or Ukraine,' he says. 'And this guy was just travelling around there with his network, producing content.' Access is the key for those wanting to exploit children, Rouse says, explaining that, 'Vulnerable families need to put food on the table.' Other evil entrepreneurs have the same modus operandi. Hundreds of other children are being forced into the same sick movie plot that Monica and Marietta were plucked from.

'It's supply and demand,' Rouse says, referring to how this is a lesson on crime and money. In 2008, superintendent Earla-Kim McColl, then head of the National Child Exploitation Co-ordination Centre in Canada, told a press conference that customers had 'sought it out, previewed the samples, paid in advance and waited for a password to download videos'.[3] Nine people were arrested in that country. Rouse says, 'I can't impact on the Sergio Marzolas of the world because I'm in Australia, except unique circumstances like this case, but I can certainly try to cut off the money. So if I start attacking the consumer, and I take out every one of these bastards who are paying money for the rape of these children, I'm doing what I can from an Australian perspective.'

8

Millie's rescue

Operation Achilles, on any judgement, was a sterling success. By the time it closed shop, dozens of people in several countries had been hauled before the courts, and a myriad child exploitation websites had been closed down. Countless children had been rescued or safeguarded from future attacks, too. Just not Millie.

Jon Rouse and his team had aged with her. They wouldn't forget her screams, or the files that outlined the abuse against her. 'Girl 1' she was called when they first came across her, but here we'll call her Millie. Then, she was just tiny, or at least that's what it seemed to investigators. But year after year, she continued to pop up in videos that ultimately sat amongst the 400 000 pieces of evidence Operation Achilles would deliver. 'We had a folder: Millie 3, Millie 4, Millie 5,' says Rouse. He didn't know her age, but he knew she celebrated about three birthdays while investigators tried to hunt down her attacker. And as she grew, so did the abuse: bondage, weapons, wielded by a predator who disguised himself, always. 'We were watching her grow up in front of us,' Rouse says. 'In one image, he's got her by the hair and he's holding a knife to her throat.' He stops, remembering how much he feared for this little girl, whose real name and location were a mystery. Because he knew that as the abuse grew, so did the chances of greater harm.

Rouse always tried to leave work at work, but this girl was the victim who kept him awake at night. 'I'd come into work thinking, What the hell am I going to see today?' he says.

The team that was trying to find Millie grew. Anders Persson from Interpol joined in. So did Paul Griffiths from the United Kingdom, and Brenden Power, Taskforce Argos's undercover operative, who pointed out any tiny reference to Millie, or any image of her, as soon as he spotted it. Warren Bulmer ignored the wishes of his boss, who wanted him to focus on national investigations, and took part from Canada. It was an elite global group. Later, Dawn Ego, a young mother who made call after call while rocking her infant child to sleep, would play a significant role. 'We basically set up to share everything we knew about this kid,' Rouse says. One problem was that, after scanning thousands of images, other children started to look like Millie. Rouse and Griffiths would disagree over a freckle on the navel of a three-year-old: Rouse thought it was Millie; Griffiths was not convinced. Everyone on that team describes feeling almost a sense of duty. This young girl was being abused year in and year out, and they hadn't been able to find her or her attacker.

Why the focus on Millie, when hundreds of other children, thousands even, were facing similar abuse? 'It was just ongoing. It was just relentless,' Rouse says. 'Sometimes cases are just a one-off. You'll see the content once. But not this.'

Over time, investigators like Bulmer filled folders of clues. The make and model of a car offered hope. A single bottle of nail polish, on the other hand, proved worthless; it was a national brand, used everywhere. There was a packet of donuts. Other images showed Millie kneeling in the back seat of a car with a box nearby displaying a partially obscured postcode. The box, with a flower on it, looked like one that might hold female products, Bulmer was told. Was it prescription medication, or something that could be purchased over the counter? He showed the box to a pharmacist in Toronto, who ruled out the possibility that it was a Canadian product. That was just one example of the many dead ends that confronted the investigators.

The car, a sunburnt-orange 2003–05 Pontiac, was a good lead, but investigators found themselves hamstrung by an inability to access every registration of that type of car – besides which, it could have been repainted. Specialists were called in to provide advice. An image showcasing a tiny piece of vegetation was studied over and over again. The predator had a permanent tan line. Did he work outdoors? Was he a farmer, perhaps? Every clue could involve weeks of pounding the pavement and phone calls, but it was crucial to build a picture of what was happening and what was irrelevant. Investigators describe it as like having a box full of jigsaw pieces, but without the lid to guide them in putting the pieces together. They didn't even know if they had all the pieces.

The crime scenes indicated Millie was being abused in several places, but a hotel room kept being featured in the images uploaded and shared around the globe. Victim identification specialists pored over the bed and the covers. Investigators zoomed in to study every square inch of the room, filling files on a single lamp, the basic furniture, even the carpet. Software was used to remove Millie from the photo so that it could be distributed far and wide, in the hope someone would pinpoint its location.

Sometimes it felt like the desperate bid to find Millie was moving forward, but then it would feel as if things were going backwards. Millie was somewhere in America, investigators were sure of that, but in a country of more than 300 million people, that didn't even amount to a single jigsaw piece – perhaps not even half of one. Rouse remembers having a feeling he'd not had before. His team wanted more clues, but that would require fresh images, and he knew that meant further abuse. It would require Millie to feel the horror of what happened each time she was taken to this nondescript hotel room. Every police investigation requires patience, particularly when there's no victim to interview or alleged offender to question, but this was tortuous: a minute or two of violence, played out on-screen, over and over again.

Victim identification was at the heart of the investigation, and that meant taking grainy hints in images and video and trying to do something with them. 'You work with what you've got,' Rouse says. Complicating matters was the fact that this offender used Photoshop to mask his face, and sometimes he'd do the same thing with his young victim. Investigators searched for something with which to identify the perpetrator: a mark on his arm, a freckle, something on his extremities. They also wanted him to speak more, so as to study his voice.

Over time, the accent of the offender did become clear. Definitely American, likely from the south-east. Rouse says if the evidence had pointed to Millie being abused in Australia, his response would have been swift. He would have removed every officer from every conceivable task, cancelled holidays and weekends, and together, they would have doorknocked every hotel in the nation. They'd set up camp in cities and in rural areas, displaying grainy photographs of a bedspread and a lamp and a piece of carpet. And every sunburnt-orange car in the country would have been waved over and inspected. But this was in another country, one with a population fifteen times larger than the one where Taskforce Argos had its offices. It was just not practical. International cooperation was strong at that time, but not ironclad like it would grow to be. So patience became Jon Rouse's unwanted friend, and each day, as different investigations spanned the globe, the crime fighters inside Taskforce Argos would reserve time to mull over what they might do next to find the little girl growing up on the screen in front of them.

The information about Millie remained scant, but the videos of abuse kept coming, distributed to a group of dark web predators. And the success of Operation Achilles wasn't getting them closer to rescuing Millie either. The effort had been a triumph, with dozens of children, just like Millie, being rescued. A couple of dozen predators were arrested in the United States, and a hundred others in nearly twenty countries. After two years, the FBI could boast the biggest digital seizure in its history. Still, says Rouse, 'I didn't want to close the operation because of Millie.' But he admits that 'we had gone as far as we possibly could, and we had to move because there are risks. We'd identified these people and it required a joint takedown globally. I remember lying on my couch, as doors were being kicked in simultaneously.'

And so, despite the accolades that flowed as Operation Achilles came to a close, none of those working on it found closure. Meanwhile, deep inside the dark web, members were seeing their network dissolve. The word was out, which meant the chances of finding Millie were becoming more and more remote. No new clues popped up. The abuse continued, but nothing appeared that would help lead investigators to the hotel room where it was happening, or the abuser who continued to steal the future of a little girl, somewhere in America.

Rouse says: 'It was a great tactical closure, but I just felt like the only thing that could help her was just heading off into the sunset.' He and the other investigators were sailing off, leaving Millie to cling to flotsam and jetsam in some overturned dinghy in the open ocean. 'It was just bloody awful.' It was the only time in my research that I saw Jon Rouse near tears.

Of course, Millie wasn't the only child left behind at the end of Operation Achilles. 'You get buried in a case, and then the next one comes and the next one and the next one and then you leave behind all of these children who have never been found,' says Rouse. 'We did everything we could at the time.' His voice trails off. He knows that the abuse of Millie continued after the case file was closed.

Before that happened, however, the team produced an intelligence flyer. It was basic, by any standard, but it included photographs of Millie and the monster they were trying to catch. In those photos, his face was painted black to hide his real appearance. In one, he was holding a knife to Millie's throat. The sunburnt-orange car was featured too. Yet another alert went out, this one through US investigators. The law enforcement realm was flooded with the details of the case. The hope was that, some day, somewhere, someone would experience a flicker of recognition, and that would end Millie's horror. For now, Jon and Paul and Anders and Warren and the team of investigators, who were all working out of a shared digital space, moved on to the next victim, the next perpetrator.

•

Dawn Ego was a new mum and a computer forensic examiner in the Maine State Police Computer Crimes Unit when a fax requesting assistance arrived. It was May 2008 – the shutters had been drawn on Operation Achilles three months earlier. Ego remembers the evening perfectly. She was pushing her infant baby in a rocker and trying to work, typing with her spare hand. When the fax came through, she was struck by the predator's face, covered in a cowardly disguise. Ego was drawn to the pictures and the information that ran alongside them. A hair bow in one of the images, in a bedroom, stood out. Her infant daughter recently had been ill, and while she was being treated at the hospital, Dawn would wander down to the maternity shop to catch her breath and a dose of fresh air. It was there that she'd seen hair bows exactly like the one in the image. 'I'd spent a lot of time in that maternity shop and it looked exactly like it,' she tells me. That night, with her baby asleep, she searched for likely manufacturers, and in a stroke of luck found that the bow in question was made by a company that only distributed to a limited number of states. 'It was a fluke, but that limited the scope from fifty states to nine or twelve,' she says. She also contacted a local botanist about a plant in one of the photos, and then revisited the photos over and over again with a fresh eye. 'In the hotel room there was a comforter,' she says. She found out everything she could about the bed quilt, then contacted the manufacturer to ask what hotel chains in her target states had been supplied with them. It came down to two states, and then she narrowed it down to Georgia, which also sold the hair bows, and a single hotel.

Ego remembers making the call: 'I actually talked to the person who cleans the room, and she said: "I know exactly. I could tell you [all about] that room."' Ego retrieved the date and time from one of the images that had been faxed to her. 'I need to know who rented that room on this particular date and time,' she told the staff member, adding: 'I wasn't sure if they were going to ask for a warrant at this point but I was prepared to go down that route if I needed to.' The staff member said the hotel had a picture of the person who had rented the room, from his licence. 'You need to send that to me,' Ego told her. She allowed herself a second of excitement. And then: 'She's like, "Sorry, the fax machine is broken," and I was like, "What? Are you kidding me? Send it to me in black and white."' It wasn't a clear photograph, but it was enough to pin down the monster. Ego also checked the vehicle that had been registered during his stay. It was a white van rather than the sunburnt-orange car, but the vehicles were linked – it later transpired that the man's wife had used the burnt-orange car on the night in question. 'At that point, I knew I had him,' says Ego. She contacted her police sergeant, who told her: 'Jesus Christ. I didn't know [you were] actually going to do it.'

Soon after, Millie was rescued. Ego says: 'I got a call in the middle of the night. And they said, "We just want to give you a heads up and let you know that the FBI did a search warrant," and they located the victim and rescued her, and the person who committed the crime admitted to everything.'

In 2009, a 39-year-old man was sentenced by US district judge Robert L Vining Jr to serve seventy years in prison on charges of producing, distributing and receiving child pornography. The man pleaded guilty, admitting both to abusing Millie and to sending out the images electronically. Millie also confirmed he had violently sexually assaulted her only hours before his arrest. US attorney David E Nahmias spoke for many when he said: 'The defendant deserves every day of the seventy-year prison sentence he received.'[1]

•

Millie's case is indelibly printed on the minds of those who lived life alongside her, searching for her. It was impossible not to look, a second time, at a child in the street. Could that be her? Or to not search for other videos in the hope of finding one more clue, seeking one tiny slip-up by the monster who was waging violence against her. Millie, and cases like hers, follow investigators home. Rouse's one-time police partner Lance Vercoe saw this in how his friend dealt with his own daughter, now an adult: 'He was extremely protective ... I would often see him being overly protective of his daughter.' Vercoe remembers at one point wanting to sit Rouse down and tell him that 'not every Catholic priest is a paedophile and not every Scout leader is trying to seduce a child'. He saw how, on occasion, Rouse would 'block everybody out', go into himself: 'We would go away fishing together. And there would be times where we would just get to the beach and he'd walk 200 metres one way and I'd walk 200 metres the other way and we just wouldn't talk.'

Rouse admits to the toll that comes with what investigators see online. And he remembers pulling himself up when he baulked at leaving his daughter with his own father, because of the role played by fathers in many of the images and videos crossing his desk: 'I said to myself, "Stop it. He's your dad and he's not going to be here for the long term." And he wasn't.' Rouse continues: 'This work changes us. Law enforcement changes you. You talk to any cop with forty years' service and they're going to say they are not the same person they were when they joined, bright-eyed and bushy tailed. We've got forty years of trauma. It's not just child abuse. It's homicide. It's road traffic command dealing with dead people in cars. I've stepped over dead bodies. I've had a seventeen-year-old overdose on drugs. We deal with trauma. If you've called us, the police, then something bad is happening.'

Rouse was in Sydney at an Interpol meeting when the text came through telling him Millie had been found. Colleagues in another country opened a bottle of champagne. But Rouse says that while everyone was cheering for the young girl, no-one was really celebrating. Rather, what washed over the investigators was an overwhelming feeling of relief.

They were aware that Millie's horror would endure in some form, with the images being traded around the globe for years to come, and some predators chasing them down on the recommendation of another. Some, Paul Griffiths says, even write letters to victims commenting on images or movies they've seen. Online, the heartache doesn't seem to end. It was also difficult for every single member of the team to know that Millie had been raped the night before her rescue.

So was this a failure, because Millie had been found well after Operation Achilles had closed? I put this question to Warren Bulmer. He says, 'No. Because at the end of the day, she was saved.' He then offers an analogy: 'When I hit a really ugly golf shot, if it gets to the green and I putt it in, all that goes on the scorecard is a number. Nobody knows how good or how bad it was. So it doesn't matter how she got rescued.' And yet, while Millie's rescue provided a happy ending for this story, he wished it had happened sooner, that better collective law enforcement decisions had prevailed earlier. He is referring to the reluctance amongst some US agencies to pull out all the stops and help investigators track Millie down. Bulmer says he even knew earlier that the perpetrator had a Georgian accent, because he'd played with footballers who spoke the same way. But he couldn't get those in America who could help, to listen. It's not said as an accusation, just an acknowledgement of the teething problems in a global effort to crack down on online child sex.

Brenden Power hints at the same thing, that sometimes investigators in different countries see things differently, and solving a case requires negotiation. Paul Griffiths says some rescues can also come down to a spot of luck: 'I could give you countless examples of the luck that we've had over the years, and you kind of make your own luck too.'

Millie was eventually ushered to safety. But the files of those who work in this area are filled with other girls just like her: young and innocent, and experiencing the depravity life can deliver before they are even old enough to begin comprehending it. And while Rouse, who trains investigators, knows it's not his job to allow any child to fill his mind beyond the investigation, he realises the struggle Millie faces to rebuild a life with a semblance of normality – despite her tormentor being sent to jail for decades. Even now, fifteen years after her rescue, he allows himself to think about her every now and again, briefly, just long enough to hope that she's found a place where she fits in, where the horror that filled her early childhood has no place. 'There's always hope,' he says. 'There's never not hope. If we gave up hope, we wouldn't keep doing the job.'

9

Will's silence

By Will's sixth birthday, he was on to his second, maybe third, passport. The smiling face of Will, who was the adopted son of Peter Truong and his American partner, Mark Newton, also filled the picture books that boasted pride of place in the family's Cairns home. At the beach. Inside his parents' immaculate home. On the manicured lawns outside. And in other places the world over. His parents seemed so damn normal, too: Truong, a Vietnamese Australian, his candid face hosting a wide open smile, and Newton, the lanky American with a receding hairline and sapphire-blue eyes. Will was Mark's biological child – both he and Peter were grateful to the Russian surrogate mother who had become pregnant almost immediately. At least, that's what they told the world in 2010. 'We're a family just like any other family,' Newton told ABC reporter Ginger Gorman.[1] The gay couple told people about their longing to have a child, and their devotion to Will stood out to those who knew the couple. 'As a reporter, you develop a pretty well-honed bullshit detector,' Gorman later wrote. 'Gut instincts are important.'[2] But nothing seemed amiss with this untraditional Far North Queensland family. Locals who knew them would later say the same: the men were devoted dads.

But as 2013 drew to a close, Newton, then forty-two, was sentenced in the United States to forty years' jail. Truong, then aged thirty-six, received a thirty-year sentence. 'This young child endured a nightmare,' United States attorney Joseph H Hogsett announced, one that stretched over three continents and included 'some of the most heinous acts of exploitation that this office has ever seen'.[3] The court found that Will's parents had travelled throughout the United States and internationally with their young son to meet with other men who then photographed Will being sexually abused. The details were monstrous.

'You want to define bad? This little boy, from the moment he was born, was sold,' says Jon Rouse. The evidence suggested Truong and Newton had systematically plotted their evil path for years beforehand, perhaps even before Will was born. 'When we dug into the financials of these two, we couldn't find a source of income,' Rouse says. Nothing really added up. The couple sold themselves as poster parents, but investigators believe they were master manipulators who bought Will for US$8000 with the intention of trafficking him around the globe. The happy family snaps were all a giant facade. 'The lies that these men told ... and they professed to love this child?' Rouse stops and just shakes his head.

On his parents' arrest in Los Angeles in 2011, Will was taken into protective custody and later placed with a family in the United States. His rescue ended one of the most psychologically challenging investigations in Taskforce Argos's history: a probe that encompassed three countries, dozens of investigators, and encrypted drives holding 25000 photographs and almost sixty-five hours of film footage. The breakthrough came in a sliding doors moment, when investigator Brian Bone from the United States Postal Inspection Service overheard a conversation as he walked down a corridor of the offices of the Child Exploitation and Obscenity Section (CEOS) of the US Department of Justice in Washington, DC.

Bone previously had worked as a detective for a sheriff's office just north of Chicago, but by the beginning of 2012, he was with the Postal Inspection Service, probing a child abuse network with tentacles in dozens of countries, including Canada and the United States. Peter Truong was listed as a member of that group, going under the pseudonym 'RedRover'. Another member of the network was found to have shared images of a young boy who was being sexually abused. There was a mole on the little boy's stomach. The conversation that Bone later overheard as he was strolling through the CEOS offices was taking place amongst several police officers and concerned a case in Australia. Drawn in by the discussion, Bone asked if he could see the images that had been sent over by Taskforce Argos. And that, he says, is when he had an 'Oh my god' moment. The child's face wasn't identifiable – clever editing had cropped his features – but Bone noted the temporary henna tattoo across his chest, and the mole on his stomach. It was just a tiny mark, the proverbial needle in a haystack of clues, but it also proved to be the crucial information that focused investigators on this child, on where they might have been and who they were with. 'It was just very incidental,' says Bone, a case of being 'in the right place at the right time thing'. In addition, while he wasn't entirely certain, images provided by Taskforce Argos of a member of the group being investigated also seemed familiar. The man looked like one of the paedophiles being tracked by his own operation.

On 2 February 2012, Bone sat down and wrote an email to Jon Rouse, care of Taskforce Argos, Queensland, the home state of the young boy we have called Will. He explained how he was investigating a 'large scale boy lover ring' that had existed since 1993, then said: 'During this investigation, we have identified the producers of numerous widely distributed child pornography services. Due to a high level of computer encryption the group was using to transmit and store their collections we indicted the known group members as part of a child exploitation enterprise.' All of the group's members had used encryption to protect their communications, but search warrants had been used to gain access to more than half of those. As a result, an attorney, who was now in custody in the United States, had been found to have molested a young victim. 'By happenchance,' says Brian Bone, that child had been identified as the adopted son of Truong and Newton.

Rouse admits it was at this point of the email, which he was reading before the sun peeked over the horizon in Brisbane, that he performed a short, solo 'happy dance' in his office. In the world of depravity in which he works, you celebrate the moments of light, however tiny. 'Holy crap,' he says. 'I come into work most days going, What am I going to be confronting today? And then I get a piece of news like that, my goodness me. We no longer had a smoking gun. We had a fire.' This was the 'Ah ha!' moment, when a breakthrough after years of work would allow a child to be rescued from the monsters who photographed his every waking moment – monsters who called themselves 'Daddy'. The clock was ticking, though. Will had been taken into care by Los Angeles authorities on the suspicions raised by investigators back in Queensland, but those working the case had been given only three months 'to come up with something', Rouse says. However, Brian Bone's email had delivered more than something. It could amount to enough evidence to charge the two men with sexual offences against the boy, as well as over their roles in the network.

Taskforce Argos officers now went back through the images taken from Truong and Newton's Cairns home. And they were able to identify the man who was captured on camera abusing the young boy.

•

The investigation into Will's case, codenamed Operation Conduit, had started much earlier with a tip-off from the New Zealand Departmental of Internal Affairs. The arrest of a man in New Zealand over the possession of child abuse material had revealed a cache of other images that stirred the interest of officers: a series of photographs and videos that, while not illegal, could perhaps be considered improper. They seemed almost professional – in the words of one investigator, they were not images 'you'd imagine a parent would take'. The child in the photographs was anonymous, with no obvious relationship to the man who'd been arrested. A car with Queensland registration plates sat in the background of one of the images, and another two men featured in the films. 'We've just pinched this guy,' an NZ officer told Rouse in a phone call, then explained that they had these images that didn't prove anything, but perhaps it was prudent to look into the background of the two men captured on film, and did Rouse want the images sent over?

Rouse and his team studied the images and came to the same conclusion as their NZ colleague. 'We were thinking, they're not the kind of photos a parent would necessarily take of their child,' says Rouse. 'And what was the child's relationship to the two men? We don't have any fire at this stage; just smoke.' Investigators swiftly identified the two men. Peter Truong was an Australian citizen, born in May 1977 in Vietnam, who now called Kewarra Beach, Cairns his home. Mark Jonathan Newton was born in December 1970 in California and carried dual Australian–US citizenship, and he also called the address in Kewarra Beach home. Both listed IT, graphic design, the internet and photography as amongst their interests. 'We're just doing background work here,' Rouse says. A small child also pops up in this research. Born in July 2005 in Rybinsk, Russia, he resides at the same address as the two men. Rouse's team digs a bit deeper, not yet overly suspicious, but wanting to know more. And they find, based on arrival cards for Brisbane airport, that the couple, carrying an infant child, had once drawn the attention of Customs staff. They had travelled together to the Queensland capital but hadn't acknowledged each other at the baggage carousel – Truong had stood by himself while Newton held the infant several metres away. This odd behaviour piqued the interest of the experienced Customs staff. They questioned Truong, who said he was travelling alone. But then he did an about-face, admitting he was accompanied by his partner, Newton, and an infant. Other discrepancies came up, but nothing that could be taken further. Newton, Truong and Will continued on their journey home.

Their lie continued for years, with the couple publicly telling the media they were gay dads and Will was their son. Investigators added that to the folder marked 'Truong and Newton'.

Meanwhile, New Zealand detectives were focused on their original arrest. A deep dive into what lay hidden behind a protected Excel spreadsheet unearthed communications between Newton, Truong and a series of other men known as 'boy lovers'. The members of what proved to be a closed network talked about boys being raised for sex, child-swap sessions, and how the Cairns couple's next trip would be to Europe, probably Germany. It was now as clear as daylight that Will was to be swapped with another boy for sex. A trip to America was also on the agenda for the following year. There, Newton and Truong would bunk down with like-minded group members – and, again, Will would be with them. 'We've got flames starting to burn now,' Rouse says.

Enter Sharon Lunn, an intelligence analyst with the Queensland-based team. Lunn had been a sworn police officer for six years back in the 1970s before leaving the service and helping out her police husband in small stations around the state. She later rejoined the force as a civilian intelligence analyst. 'Jon was the best police officer I've ever worked with,' says Lunn, who is now retired. 'I don't think you would have a figure for the number of kids that [Rouse and Taskforce Argos] have saved. And not only Australian kids. As soon as we found out that there was a child at risk, you'd be dealing with a country that would work with us. Sometimes those children were rescued within minutes.' She falls silent for a moment. 'But it breaks your heart when you know you haven't saved them.' Lunn goes on to say that Rouse and Paul Griffiths, whom colleagues say boasts a photographic memory that allows him to recall an image from years earlier, made the perfect partnership: 'It would give me the shits at times. You worked so hard, and [Griffiths] would take one look and say, "That's already been identified, so don't do anymore on that because it's a waste of time."' Her mockery is light-hearted – Sharon Lunn believes the work done by Rouse and Griffiths to save children makes them both saints.

Griffiths' memory is brought up several times during my research for this book. 'It's something I've always had,' he tells me, without a skerrick of a gloat, adding that perhaps this ability has become sharper through his job. 'I remember things as a photograph,' he says. 'So the reason I can tell you where something's located or how to find whatever it might be, is because I can see it.'

Lunn remains coy about how she analysed the intelligence around Newton and Truong. She plucks out words. Travel. Money. Registration plates. Phone calls. Places. Maps. Charts. But she won't be drawn on exactly what transpired. That modus operandi stays with police, she says. Neither Truong nor Newton had any criminal history. But when associates' names are checked with investigators overseas, they find one is under investigation by the FBI for the distribution of child abuse material, another is in custody in Germany awaiting trial on child abuse charges, and yet another is a top-ranked capital markets lawyer and partner in an international firm who is also facing child abuse charges but has been released on bail after payment of a $250000 bond. A sharply focused picture is emerging. In one encoded internet communication, a father admits that his own son has watched Will being sexually abused. Investigators talk to that boy and he tells them of a visit by another boy with 'two dads and no mother', and recognises him immediately. This is more than enough for Taskforce Argos to conduct on-the-ground surveillance back in Cairns. When they find out that Newton and Truong have left for the United States, investigators head to the sleepy, family-filled suburb of Kewarra Beach.

The first thing they notice at the suspects' home are the security cameras – they're everywhere, monitoring visitors from every angle. Investigators know if they cut the power to cover their entry into the house, Newton and Truong might be alerted. So they check with neighbours, who confirm that they are acting as the couple's point of contact while they're overseas. Under the guise of remedying a power outage, but secretly equipped with a search warrant, the officers gain access. Truong and Newton, on the other side of the globe, are notified their security has been switched off and check back with their neighbours, and they believe the power-outage story they are told. Once inside, what stands out to investigators are the homemade picture books documenting travels around the world. A passport in Will's name, full of stamps, also raises a flag.

The boy has now left the country again, presumably with another passport, so how much has this child travelled in a few short years? Hard drives are found, too. And a strip of photographic negatives stapled to the back of a book. Truong's fingerprints are on those negatives, which include the photograph of an unidentified naked boy. 'We've got enough for an arrest at that point,' Rouse says, adding: 'Joe Blow would have a gut feeling by now.'

On the back of Argos's concerns, Truong and Newton are detained by the Los Angeles Police Department. Will is questioned by an FBI forensic interviewer. It's 19 October 2011. The interviewer's report later says: 'Based on my training and experience, as well as the training and experience of expert trial forensic interviews with both [the] Department of Homeland Security and FBI, it is extremely common for victims of sexual abuse not to disclose the abuse during the initial interview.' This is not surprising. An abused child mostly wants to protect their parents, and often has been groomed to answer pesky questions in a particular way. And so it proves – investigators reveal Will was often driven past a prison in Far North Queensland and told that's where his parents would end up if something went wrong. Will admits during the interview that he knows those associates of his parents who are currently on trial or being investigated over child abuse. The six-year-old doesn't disclose any abuse. 'However, the manner in which Will answered the questions could indicate that he has been coached not to answer them,' reports the interviewer. 'For instance, when he was asked about non sexual matters, Will was bright and responsive. When he was asked questions that could lead to a discussion of sexual abuse however,

Will hid his face, did not want to answer the questions and expressed concern that one of his fathers would go to jail.'

Rouse says the silence of an abused child always makes his work more difficult. Some fear their truth will mean the only family they have will be taken away from them. Others believe there is a sense of 'normalcy' around their relationship with an abuser. Others don't know that what has been happening is wrong, or carry a sense of shame. And still others cannot find the words to outline the nightmare they are living. In this case, Will's refusal or inability to reveal the horrors he faced meant his parents were released from custody, having refused to be interviewed by police. But then comes a reprieve for Rouse – Los Angeles authorities agree to Will being placed in the care of the city's Department of Children and Family Services for three months while detectives try to unlock encrypted hard drives and decode messages sent through the dark web. 'The clock is now seriously ticking,' Rouse says.

Newton and Truong take their case to the media. 'An Australian gay couple have had their six-year-old son taken from them by child protection authorities in LA while the FBI and Queensland police investigate allegations that they are members of an international paedophile ring,' one Australian report read.[4] Truong and Newton claimed they were innocent, the victims of 'prejudice in Australia and the US against gay fathers'. They said they had been unknowingly caught up in wrongdoing after 'innocent visits to three men in the US, New Zealand and Germany, who to their complete surprise, turned out to be collectors and producers of child pornography'. All three of those men had been arrested the previous year. Asked by the media to explain 'their serial contact with child pornographers', they responded that they were simply three out of twenty men they knew, asserting: 'We would never hurt our child.' It was, of course, all lies.

At this point, it was evidence that counted. Enter Griffiths, the one-time UK detective who joined Taskforce Argos on Rouse's invitation. He has a massive task in front of him, sifting through 300000 images and 5200 videos.[5] 'I viewed all the photographs and watched all the video,' Griffiths says. His job was to build a picture of the couple's real relationship with Will. 'It would have been nice to have evidence of offending against the child,' he says, but that wasn't found in the men's home. 'What we did have was innocent photographs that were taken in strange locations,' continues Griffiths. 'So they were obviously travelling the world, and one of the things I did was I stuck all the locations onto a spreadsheet and started mapping where they were on which dates.' That provided an expansive chronology of where Truong and Newton had travelled, who they had met and who had featured in the images.

Griffiths practically dismisses his efforts as all part of a day's work, but the sheer workload was almost unmanageable, taking up every waking moment for weeks on end. Unfortunately, while two registered sex offenders in the United Kingdom pop up, the work doesn't deliver what is needed to show evidence of Truong or Newton sexually abusing their child. Griffiths' work is bundled up and forwarded to CEOS in the US Department of Justice. Perhaps in America, where Truong and Newton are spending so much of their time, and where many of the members of their closed group reside, other clues might surface.

Brian Bone was busy assisting with Operation Spade, a probe that began in 2010 in Toronto. By any standard, that investigation was colossal, eventually touching on more than fifty countries and leading to the rescue of more than 350 children.[6] Primary producers of the illegal content were found in Germany, Romania and Ukraine. Operation Spade evolved into many other operations, including one based around the southern districts of Indiana, where a small group of individuals had launched a group to exploit children. And that, not the Australian operation, was Bone's focus. But sometimes, luck favours the brave, and that's how Bone sees the events that allowed him to deliver the news about Will to Jon Rouse.

Bone didn't know Rouse personally at the time, but he knew of Argos's standing in the online child sex investigation world. His primary partners in his own investigation, the Toronto police, had worked with Argos on other cases. 'I wouldn't say that it's a small world, but it's a very cooperative world,' he says. 'So when you have something like this [the photograph of Will], you feel very comfortable to reach out to whatever entity it is because everybody has the same goal – to rescue children.' Bone praises that unique teamwork, something that other law enforcement agencies can struggle with because of competing interests. 'Within the child exploitation realm, there's no competing interests,' explains Bone. 'The interest is to be able to save children.' Indeed, this single case involved a number of law enforcement bodies: the New Zealand Department of Internal Affairs, several US agencies, German authorities and Taskforce Argos. While the FBI is the predominant federal law enforcement agency in the United States, there are many others at work in the country, and the Postal Inspection Service is one of the oldest. It has been that way 'pretty much since the start of the nation because the founding fathers had realised that they needed to protect the mail being delivered', explains Bone proudly, a fifteen-year employee of the agency.

Bone says that having these global connections is what solves tricky investigations. 'If we had all been working in a vacuum, we wouldn't have been able to put two and two together,' he says. Both Bone and Taskforce Argos had hit a roadblock in their respective investigations until that sliding doors moment when Brian Bone overheard a simple conversation, pursued it, and identified Will.

•

Will's parents were charged on 23 February 2012, with evidence being given that the boy was made available for sex to at least eight men in America and Europe, when he was aged between two and six. 'This is not a case that lends itself to easy understanding,' said US District Court judge Sarah Evans Barker.[7] The facade was down, and the pixels on those perfect photographs were seen close up. Newton was shackled before the court, and when he spoke his voice shook. Being a father, he said, had been an 'honour and a privilege' that amounted to the best six years of his life.[8] 'Words don't help,' Barker responded.[9] Newton and Truong had gone to great lengths to acquire a child from a mother in Russia before brainwashing him to think abuse was normal, she said.[10]

Hetty Johnston, who founded Bravehearts, says she has 'no words' to describe Truong and Newton, who masqueraded as role-model parents. 'They should get life ... never to be released ... all their assets given to the organisations fighting the sexual assault and exploitation of children. They are the lowest of the low.'

Rouse says investigators will never know what story Will's parents spun to a child who deserved so much more. Neither does he know how Will is faring now, but he keeps his fingers crossed that Will has been able to reach an adolescence that's brought a sense of closure. Rouse has not sought him out: 'I can't concern myself any further, except to know that he was okay.' But don't you worry about that, I ask? It's the only time Jon Rouse bites back at one of my questions: 'Of course I do. But I don't think about it, because it would tear me apart. If we worried about these kids after what we've done, we couldn't work. I couldn't function.'

Rouse will admit he's pleased that Newton and Truong were tried in the United States, where the penalties for their crimes routinely stretch well beyond a normal life sentence. 'Justice was served,' he says. And just in case either of those men believe that freedom awaits, Taskforce Argos still has the file open. They have that negative, with the unidentified naked boy, and a fingerprint. And they're ready.

10

A homegrown monster

It was after dark one Tuesday evening in June 2014 when Shannon Grant McCoole, a 32-year-old childcare worker, answered a knock on the front door of his home in the southern Adelaide suburb of Oaklands Park. Detective Sergeant Stephen Hegarty from South Australian Police was carrying a general search warrant as he stepped inside the government worker and volunteer's modest, messy home, followed by two Taskforce Argos members. The three investigators knew that McCoole was the international administrator of an insidious child abuse network termed The Love Zone, the man atop a hierarchy that encouraged and facilitated the abuse of children across the globe.

An unsuspecting McCoole was gobsmacked. Hegarty had wanted to catch McCoole off guard, so as to not allow him time to slam shut his laptop – thousands of leads lay behind the passwords and membership rules that served as the dark web gateway to The Love Zone. Sure enough, when the officers spotted McCoole's computer, crucial links sat open, like big brassy headlines, and the hard drive would prove to contain a backup of the entire site. This access would allow investigators to sneak through another door, and by doing so not only send McCoole to jail for decades, but also spark a royal commission in South Australia, highlight the complex and sophisticated structures set up online to hide abuse, and fan new investigations across the globe. But above all, when the file closed on The Love Zone investigation several years later, almost seventy children had been rescued, numerous offenders had been arrested, and a total of 180 targets referred to other law enforcement agencies.

The impetus for McCoole's arrest had begun four years earlier in a warehouse in Toronto, where a customer base for a production company was stored. Thousands of videos were found, mostly of nude boys from Ukraine. That investigation was long and arduous, but it rescued more than 300 children a long way from Australia. Amongst those fat customer base files were thirty-seven Queensland targets – men who had signed up to receive images and videos. 'We arrested thirty-four here,' says Jon Rouse. 'We made one-tenth of the world's arrests just in Queensland.' One of those was a Brisbane man called Mr Smith. When Taskforce Argos officers arrived at Smith's home, an unkempt property in the northern suburb of Banyo, they found their target hiding in bushes dressed in camouflage gear.

Rouse tells that story almost as an aside. That's because he and his officers knew that the real story, as with all online sexual predators, lay in what they might find on a laptop or computer in Smith's home. Their intelligence suggested that he was a VIP subscriber on a Tor board called The Love Zone. And that fact sparked an investigation – called

Operation Rhodes – that was still making headlines a decade later.

•

At the heart of any international child exploitation racket is a structure, carefully organised in the same way a company might be set up; none of it is haphazard. The Love Zone was a stellar example of this. Members earned trust by meeting entry rules, one of which required them to regularly upload abhorrent images using special software that hid their identity. The authenticity of the uploads was then checked. Those in management positions were cautious, knowing law enforcement wanted to infiltrate their network and close them down. It was a game of chess with real-life consequences.

While the international administrator was at the apex of the management pyramid, there were four other website administrators. Below them were co-administrators, and under those people were 'moderators'. Together, they were the 'admin team'. McCoole determined the role of each admin member – moderators, for example, checked that any posts met the proscribed rules. 'Members were sanctioned if the rules were not obeyed. Sanctions included warnings, temporary bans, permanent bans and deletion,' reported the 2015 Queensland Organised Crime Commission of Inquiry.[1] Admin team members had access to all areas of the site, while for others, the degree of access depended on which membership class they belonged to: registered member, full member, VIP member or other member. There were also two parts of the site with restricted access. The first was the private zone, reserved for new or rare content. 'To gain access, lower status members were required to post their new or rare content, and existing private zone members would vote to decide whether it was new or rare enough to grant membership,' said the commission of inquiry. 'Members of the private zone were required to post every 14 days to maintain their membership of that private zone.' The second area was the producers' lounge, for members who were producing their own content. The commission of inquiry revealed that: 'In order to gain access to the producer's [sic] lounge, a member must have proven that he or she has access to at least one child, and the ability to produce content involving that child.' Videos needed to run for five minutes, or alternatively 100 images needed to be provided. A child also needed to 'hold a sign that had the applicant's user name and the date and particular words for further authentication of the production'.[2]

Mr Smith's online activity was towards the lower end of all this, but it was still high enough for him to maintain VIP status. On Smith's arrest, Taskforce Argos sought permission to run a 'controlled' operation which permits a covert officer to commit criminal activity for the purposes of gaining evidence and identifying offenders. When this was granted, Smith's identity was quickly assumed, his account taken over by a covert police agent. That wasn't burdensome: Smith was not well known and didn't have idiosyncrasies that stood out to others communicating with him. The undercover police officer simply had to maintain a presence and comply with membership rules.

Officers raced to gather evidence, all of which was abhorrent: manuals on how users could lure children into their net, how to abuse children, and how not to get caught. The collection of this evidence was only possible because members didn't know that one of their own was now spying on them – their messages and videos, images and chat were being monitored by a covert operative from Taskforce Argos. That undercover work prompted dozens of leads that were passed on to law enforcement agencies in several countries. In Australia, they led straight to the person in charge of the operation, the global administrator, who used the name 'Skee'. 'He was the boss. He was the self-pronounced head honcho,' Rouse says. 'And under him was this criminal organisation infrastructure. And I can say that because there were members who were vetting the uploads to make sure that they met criteria. There were new applicants for membership. ... There were members of the board who were responsible for security. This was organised crime, and the commodity was children.'

The covert operator engaged with Skee, pretending he was one of The Love Zone members – an abuser who went deep inside the dark web to swap images and videos of children. It was a high-risk play. A single slip-up might prompt the whole network – which had 45 000 members – to close, allowing the individuals to move on to another dark web club. And that would mean children would continue to be raped, and images of those crimes would continue to be traded online as some sort of sordid currency. This effort was mammoth and global, and it focused Taskforce Argos's attention twenty-four hours a day.

Those who participate in any child sex exploitation, online or offline, go to extraordinary lengths to hide it. Some are drawn to careers where access to children is easy because it offers a cover for their filthy activities. Police officers and businessmen, teachers and Scout leaders, priests and volunteer workers have all been apprehended on child sex charges, as in Operation Auxin. So taking over Smith's account was a significant first step, because it allowed police to see the size of the network's membership, as well as its modus operandi. But finding Skee, the kingpin, was pivotal. One post strongly pointed to him being an Australian and running the global network from his home country. But where specifically in Australia might he be? And who was he offline? Was he a teacher, responsible for a class of children? Unemployed? An IT worker? A businessman, savvy with a computer? Skee was certainly careful, making sure during each online conversation not to present the undercover agent, or any other member, with anything that might pinpoint his identity.

Patience is an investigator's friend, however, and eventually a few clues appeared in the personal uploads Skee offered members. The first was a freckle on one of his fingers. It wasn't huge, but it was visible, and every image of it was studied. The second was a mark on Skee's penis. Neither of those clues would help police find Skee, but once they had located him, these identifying marks would assist in confirming the evidence gathered against him. And so the parallel investigations continued to run, covertly and overtly. Interpol and other police teams scoured sites and communications, and shared information and tips, slowly building a picture of the club's boss. On some days investigators thought they were sliding backwards; on other days there would be cyber high-fives as a tiny tip promised new hope.

It was a quirk in the way Skee spoke that eventually undid him. An aspect of his personality that he showed in the dark web put him in plain sight of Paul Griffiths, the victim identification specialist, and it came down to one letter. Skee had an unusual greeting for members. He used the word 'Hiyas', with an 's' on the end. It was never 'Hi you' or 'Hi ya', always 'Hiyas'. It struck Griffiths as unusual and led him down investigative rabbit holes. A fake Facebook account popped up via a circuitous exploration, which then led to an innocuous four-wheel-drive forum. Everything pointed to a male who was employed by the South Australian Government as a childcare worker. A vehicle registration plate on a Facebook page completed the picture and took Stephen Hegarty and two members of Taskforce Argos to Shannon McCoole's front door.

It's impossible not to like Griffiths. He's disarming, a straight shooter, and he's committed to finding children who are in harm's way. His job in victim identification means the father of two sees the worst of humankind, but he talks about the three or so emails he receives each week detailing how victims have been found as a result of leads provided by Taskforce Argos in Australia – young girls and boys, somewhere in the world, who have been removed from unimaginable danger. He also admits he kicked himself when he found out McCoole's job. Offenders like McCoole often choose jobs where they are able to access children, and Griffiths says he 'couldn't understand why I hadn't realised that he was a childcare worker. He had a number of children he was offending against who were clearly not family members.' But, he says, 'even if I had realised that, I don't know that he would have been any easier to find'.

•

Leads generated by Taskforce Argos's infiltration of Skee's Love Zone continued to garner results around the world. One of these was centred on Richard William Huckle, a serial child sex offender who has since been labelled Britain's worst paedophile. Huckle was born in 1986 in Ashford, Kent, to a middle-class family. A regular churchgoer, he was described as a 'loner', but nothing in his early life stood out as a big red alert for the sordid activities he would later pursue. In his mid-twenties, Huckle moved to Malaysia, a country he was familiar with because of regular visits to assist local churches. He gained work as a freelance photographer, and was employed by sporting clubs and at an orphanage in Bangalore, India. Huckle stood out to Taskforce Argos investigators – though they were yet to learn his name – soon after they assumed McCoole's account. The number of children abused by this individual, as evidenced by the material uploaded to The Love Zone, was striking. This man was just one sub-investigation out of dozens and dozens, but the access he had to children, and his secret posts, prompted urgent and deeper digging. It didn't take long for his real identity to surface – and the fact that he was due to return home to Britain to spend Christmas with his family.

Huckle was met by law enforcement officers at Gatwick Airport six days before Christmas in 2014. He was granted bail as police continued to delve into his history of abusing young children, during which time he lived with his parents, who confronted him over those accusations. He admitted to them that he'd raped young children, and they alerted police – then promptly disowned him. Huckle's string of offences was so long that it would take more than an hour to read out the list of charges at his first appearance at London's Old Bailey in early 2016. The details were heartbreaking and included the rape and digital penetration of young children, the creation of child abuse material, and the possession and distribution of child pornography, to name but a few. He'd also produced a 'child lover guide' that sat alongside his abuse of children aged six months to twelve years. In it, he boasted that 'impoverished kids are definitely much easier to seduce than middle-class kids', and that he had 'hit jackpot' with a toddler who was as 'loyal to me as my dog'.[3] No-one knows how many children fell victim to Huckle, but estimates range from twenty-three to 169. He was sentenced to life imprisonment. Three years later, in October 2019, Huckle was stabbed to death in prison.

While Huckle's case was playing out in the United Kingdom, other abusers were being arrested and tried across Canada, Europe and Australia. Children were being rescued as national agencies focused on key targets in their own jurisdictions. Back in South Australia, meanwhile, McCoole had been caught red-handed. A freckle on his right ring finger confirmed to the investigators now standing in his lounge room that they had The Love Zone's big boss. And the look on his face showed them he knew his secret was now public. McCoole signed over his online identities to Taskforce Argos, allowing two covert officers to tag team around the clock, disguised as the site's chief administrator, its CEO – a huge step up from pretending to be Mr Smith, a run-of-the-mill member of the club with no online decision-making role. This meant they needed to be in perfect sync, slipping into the role of McCoole's cyber-ego, Skee, without making other members suspicious, certainly without revealing that their leader was now sitting in a jail cell in Adelaide. Both agents were careful to ensure they reflected Skee's speech and the limited personality he had shared with members. But it also meant that a secret online club whose aim was to sexually exploit children in the most hideous ways deep inside the dark web would now be administered by law enforcement. It was uncharted territory. Taskforce Argos operatives had previously played the role of online paedophiles, but Skee was the top guy, commanding an operation that involved engaging with 45 000 offenders.

The use of undercover operatives in crime detection is discussed in Chapter 11, including the criticism levelled at Taskforce Argos during Operation Artemis. I might have joined those criticisms before researching this book. But ask any respected senior crime fighter and they will explain how covert operations are the only way in which serious criminal activity, like the rape of young children and the sharing of footage of this, can be detected, and the evidence for prosecution collected. These crimes aren't committed out in the open but occur behind closed doors, often directed by someone a child trusts, and the proof lies almost exclusively in the images swapped on the dark web. Like undercover drug operatives in other police units, online child sex abuse investigators need to take on the persona of a paedophile to get this evidence.

Beyond carefully adhering to the laws governing covert operations, Rouse says the question he has always asked himself is whether his team's actions are publicly defensible – and he can't imagine anyone thinking they aren't when the stakes are so high. Rescuing children – those whose young faces fill the screens in his day-to-day work – is the top priority.

Ultimately, what this all meant in the McCoole case was that police were now running the club. Their engagement had gone from pretending to be a VIP member under Mr Smith's pseudonym, with limited access to the dark web site, to controlling the operation, acting as the CEO of a global criminal network. It also meant they now had access to every secret room in the club, where offending was produced on demand. Taskforce Argos set about de-anonymising as many of those 45 000 members as possible, downloading the evidence that would allow them to be charged in the jurisdictions where they lived. It also closed the club to all new members, and shut the producers' lounge. But for Operation Rhodes, a big piece of the jigsaw remained missing. Skee was the club's administrator, but he did not 'host' the site. 'We needed to find out where the hell the server was located,' Rouse says.

Leads soon pointed to the hosting entity, who went by the moniker of IOH ('I'm Only Human'), and a combination of investigative work and other clues unearthed IOH's address in the Netherlands – which was immediately put under old-fashioned traditional surveillance by the country's police. The next step was crucial. While Argos was authorised to take over accounts, controlled operations protocols required any targeted sites to be hosted in Australia, so The Love Zone site needed to be found and imported to within Australia's borders. One of Skee's covert impersonators now engaged with IOH. At first it was mindless banter, including discussion of *Game of Thrones*. But then the agent asked IOH for a backup of The Love Zone files in their entirety. IOH, who believed he was speaking to the club's administrator, began transferring the backup through the ether to Australia, onto a Taskforce Argos computer. After what probably felt like an eternity to the agent, but which was probably only a matter of minutes, the download was complete. And by then, the Dutch police, with the steps of a ballerina, had slipped into IOH's home and removed him from his keyboard. The arrest of IOH was so smooth that the Australia-based agent kept talking after it had occurred, unaware no-one was listening.

IOH was now in police custody, and the site data had been obtained. The mission was complete.

•

Negotiations with Dutch prosecutors allowed Taskforce Argos to migrate The Love Zone data back to its head office, where officers readied to switch it on at the same moment it was turned off overseas. It had to be done meticulously, as a tiny glitch could raise suspicion amongst the tens of thousands of club members, who remained unaware that their nefarious postings were being caught in a police sting. Rouse takes up the story: 'And there was a glitch in the matrix and we were down for a very short amount of time.' But it was long enough to be noticed by one member, who was described by others as a bit like the brother-in-law you didn't want at the family barbecue. Krafft Ebing, as he was known online, was seen as a know-it-all. So when he alerted the rest of the group about the unusual activity, many quickly dismissed it, believing Ebing was big-noting himself. Still, police pushed Ebing up the police priority target list – they couldn't afford to be found out. He was soon located in Spain, and more than a dozen children were subsequently placed on a watchlist. It was a close call because, in sporting parlance, investigations into The Love Zone were in the home stretch. The administrator had been removed. The technology master was in custody. The server was in the hands of Taskforce Argos. And police units around the world were about to pounce on those homes where children were being abused.

A last-bid effort was made to nab as many members of the online club as possible. Remember that these members were required to regularly upload sexual exploitation material to maintain membership; if they didn't, they risked being banished. But each time they did so, they also committed an offence. A decision was made by Argos to allow a further two upload cycles, to catch those proactively uploading child sex images. A tailored software package automatically captured every detail: the time of the upload, the date, the user and the content posted. Technology was also deployed that meant a link cleverly lured members outside the dark web, and several hundred members fell for that, before others picked up on the law enforcement trick and alerted their online colleagues.

But by then, The Love Zone was in ruins: its leadership was in jail, communication channels had been closed down, and hundreds of offenders were facing court. Most importantly, sixty-eight children had been rescued. Other members escaped attention, however, and slipped off to join other clubs, which continue to grow. One called PlayPen boasted four times the number of members – 180000 individuals – only a year later.

McCoole's arrest quickly became the subject of national debate. How did he end up in a job that required he care for children? How was he vetted? What needed to change to ensure someone like Shannon McCoole was never put in charge of children again? The South Australia–based Child Protection Systems Royal Commission was established in 2014 in an attempt to address those questions, and others around the red flags and concerns that had been noted earlier in McCoole's employment.

McCoole gave evidence to that inquiry, raising more questions than answers. He later told a court that, on his release, he wanted to work with teens who had paedophilic tendencies.[4] He also told police, during an interview in jail, that he had 'hated myself for years' for what he'd done. 'I looked for help. I didn't find any. I never went to work with kids for this to happen. I didn't want this to happen. I learned from my work what these kids go through. I absolutely hate it. I decided many years ago to never do this again, but ...' McCoole went on to say he couldn't explain his actions: 'You just put it out of your mind I guess. I really don't know why.' And he made an audacious claim: 'I don't like paedophiles.' It was a spectacular about-turn from offender to self-proclaimed victim.[5]

McCoole, who was employed as a worker in child care by the South Australian Government from 2011 to 2014, was convicted of a range of sex offences against seven children – boys and girls aged between eighteen months and three years. More than 50000 images involving children were found on his computer. The details of his offending are truly sickening. Most of his victims were in the care of the state. He was sentenced to a jail term of thirty-five years.

Is he now sitting in jail rotting, and feeling sorry for himself? Or is he thinking he needs to make amends for what he did? These questions, posed by Jon Rouse, are rhetorical. Rouse shakes his head. He watched an arrogant, even haughty criminal CEO called Skee turn himself into a hard-done-by carer and victim from Adelaide. And like other experts in this area, he doesn't believe a word of it.

Part 4

Searching for clues

11

Covert cops

Martin Scorsese's crime thriller *The Departed* is enthralling. It's not just the star-studded cast – headlined by Jack Nicholson, Matt Damon and Leonardo DiCaprio – but also the pace of the movie, the twists and turns as Damon's and DiCaprio's characters rise through the ranks of a group drenched in organised crime and headed by Nicholson. But the clincher is that one is an undercover police officer, the other an undercover criminal masquerading as a police officer. To say more would be a spoiler.

On a movie set, undercover work, like most police work, can be portrayed with glamour. Away from the set, the life of a covert police operative runs to a completely different script. It's lonely, built on falsehoods that can cost friendships and families. It means living a lie, climbing out of bed each morning and acting on a crime stage where a tiny mistake in method acting can cost the undercover actor or a citizen their life. It means driving home a different way each week, or living in caravans and hotels out of suitcases, hypervigilant that the backstory, carefully scripted to allow the infiltration of a criminal network, never ever slips.

Keith Banks has always been a keen martial artist, and as a 22-year-old it was taekwondo he practised. At the time, everyone knew he was a police officer. He remembers the first sentence of the script that launched his two years on the streets, masquerading as a drug dealer. 'I went [to taekwondo] one night and announced I'd been fired from the police force because they found dope in my locker,' he says. He still remembers the raised eyebrows, the looks: 'All of my friends thought I was a disgraced cop for almost two years.' Night and day for the next twenty-four months, Banks lived the life of a drug dealer. He copied the language and the clothes, the idiosyncrasies of those who owned the streets in Brisbane, the Gold Coast and Cairns. 'My role was to buy drugs, essentially from dealers,' he says. 'Part of that was to masquerade as a dealer without actually selling drugs.' His cover was that he had a set market but was in search of a better supply. He told his new drug associates, who he would later testify against in court, that he didn't touch the stuff himself. He only wanted to make money.

Banks says he didn't receive a scrap of training but learned as he worked the streets. By the time he moved into the heroin world, he'd been an undercover operative for just six months. 'I'd learned how to act. My favourite analogy is that it's like NIDA [National Institute of Dramatic Art], but on steroids. You had to be a method actor. You had to really understand it.' That's because the people he was involved with would mete out a severe beating or even murder if they believed their close-knit crime syndicate had been infiltrated by law enforcement. 'The danger was from being outed as a cop. But it was also as dangerous if not more to be ripped off because we always had cash and in the drug world, there is no loyalty,' says Banks.

He remembers being on edge the whole time. It wasn't a day job – he lived it for twenty-four hours each day. In small towns, his accomplices knew his home was a hotel room, so that meant he could never drop his disguise. On one occasion he was warned he needed to 'lay low' for a couple of weeks, so he went to visit his mother, a day's drive from his drug beat. She opened the door, viewed the long-haired, unshaven character in front of her, and didn't show a flicker of recognition. In operations in Brisbane, it was a modicum easier. Banks lived at home and could shut his door and forget it all – until the next day. But only after he took a circuitous route home, to make sure he was not being followed. Banks's return to uniform drew a mixed response. His taekwondo class applauded him. His hairdresser, a female peer he was smitten with, was genuinely offended: 'She cut my hair and never spoke to me again.'

Former undercover officer Stacey Kirmos's story follows a similar script. Lauded as one of Australia's best covert operatives, he spent nine years in the company of armed robbers, drug dealers and murderers. His ability to act, he says, was driven by the necessity to stay alive: 'I started acting like a crim. I picked up habits off crims. I just copied some of these people.' He couldn't tell friends what he did, and some of those relationships fell away. Unable to talk about his role with those he loved most, he says he parted ways with his family, too. But the convictions he secured could not have been achieved in any other way. They included the arrest of a woman who hired him to kill her husband. 'I went and met the wife and we had conversations, and eventually it all ended up where I was going out, and she was meeting me on the day to pay me and I was gonna go and kill her husband,' he says.

My search for undercover operatives outside the area of sexual assault was prompted by criticism levelled at Taskforce Argos, particularly during Operation Artemis. The eleven-month infiltration of a huge global online paedophile network drew the ire of some academics and journalists. The details of that will follow, but first, what is the role of a covert officer? Where are the guidelines that dictate what they can do and what they can't? And would it be possible to pick up a child sex abuser, deep inside the web, without becoming one of them?

Kirmos says when a criminal makes a decision to commit or conceal a crime, that line fades. 'I never pushed a person to sell me drugs,' he says. 'They were dealing with drugs. They were dealing in robberies. They were dealing in murders and all sorts of offences. With me, or without me, they would have still gone ahead.' Keith Banks, whose book *Drugs, Guns and Lies* was published in 2020, says electronic taps, social media and other modern-day innovations can help solve serious crime. 'But an undercover cop immerses himself or herself in that criminal world and once you gain the trust of people, you will get more information and more evidence than you ever would by traditional means,' he says. The challenge of undercover policing, explains Banks, lies in 'retaining your moral compass and a sense of who you are'. However, he says that he would struggle to do the work of the undercover agents assigned to Taskforce Argos: 'The stress. The pressure.

The emotional torment. All that stuff. I take my hat off to them. If it wasn't for undercover operatives, paedophiles would be running rampant, because there wouldn't be that ability to masquerade as a fourteen-year-old kid to come in and take the bait.'

Taskforce Argos operatives, like undercover agents in other criminal areas, are governed by legislation. As mentioned earlier, controlled operations are overseen by police powers and responsibilities laws, as well as legislation concerning sex offences. And so it is in other jurisdictions, with laws decided by parliament setting the parameters within which covert operators can infiltrate crime groups and gather evidence. In short, this legislation is aimed at allowing undercover officers to interact with criminals in a bid to extract both information and evidence. In Queensland, where Taskforce Argos is headquartered, it is lawful for an officer to hide their true identity, and, according to the Queensland Organised Crime Commission of Inquiry, 'acts committed by the officer that would otherwise be unlawful are deemed lawful if committed under the prescribed circumstances'.[1] Other jurisdictions within Australia, and around the world, have similar controls.

A couple of decades ago, before the aforementioned Queensland law was enacted, it was Jon Rouse who helped write a submission to allow covert activity. He then handed it to his boss, who took it to a committee that acts as the arbiter of such things to this day. It was inspector Annie Macdonald, who appointed Rouse to Taskforce Argos, who was a stickler for having the legislative support for covert operations. 'We had to make sure that what we did was beyond reproach,' she tells me. 'There could be no ramifications coming back saying that this was done wrongly. Once we started, everything had to be done to the letter of the law.' In the early days, that proved difficult, especially when the resources of Google were not a keystroke away. 'We would have people sitting on the floor and you might have the target asking what particular colour [school] uniform [does our operative] wear,' says Macdonald. That would prompt a lot of scurrying in an attempt to find someone who could answer that specific question. But while that kind of information is easier to track down now, the speed and sophistication of online communication means it is now also much easier to make a mistake.

While today's police undercover work has been governed in the same way for more than two decades, each year Rouse or members of his team – just as happens with peers in other parts of the police service – are required to front up and answer any questions posed by the approval committee, which always includes a judicial officer. This is an attempt to stem the controversy around the use of undercover agents – controversy that in some cases has wound up in the High Court. It has drawn fire in Argos's case too. Keith Banks understands that using evidence gained from undercover work is considered by the defence in court as 'unfair'. But he says it is 'just as unfair to hamstring police by not having an ability to actually gain evidence that will convict'. This is the case whether police are trying to arrest an armed robber or track down a child sex offender. 'It's about the end result, which is obtaining evidence to have an offender charged and convicted and jailed,' Banks says.

At the end of the day, it comes down to public opinion: the pub test. Do law-abiding citizens, going about their day, support the use of operatives to nab baddies? It was Operation Artemis, which focused on two big dark web clubs – the Giftbox Exchange and Child's Play – that turned that question into a media headline.

•

In mid-2016, Taskforce Argos was given a gift by overseas law enforcement officers: the account details and passwords of the moderator of the Giftbox Exchange site. While some claim this occurred because it was easier to infiltrate such networks under the law that governed Argos, there was a direct nexus with Australia involving crypto-payments to an Australian reseller. Argos had for some time been touted as being amongst the world's top child sex crime fighters. It had punched above its weight in operation after operation, drawing the accolades of peers in the United States, Europe and Canada. So it was routine, by this stage, to knock on the digital door of this unit. Sure enough, Argos discovered that another dark web club called Child's Play seemed to link to the Giftbox Exchange. And that led investigators to a man whose online persona was 'Warhead'. Offline, he was a Canadian called Benjamin Faulkner.

In 2019, Faulkner and his chief co-accused, Patrick Falte, from Tennessee, would plead guilty and be sentenced in the US District Court to thirty-five years' jail each. They and two others were also sentenced to a lifetime of supervised release, after the court heard they set up and ran a global child exploitation enterprise. Falte and Faulkner also faced another life sentence, delivered two years earlier, for the repeated sexual abuse of a toddler. US crime fighters saw the jailing of these offenders as a big win. 'The Giftbox Exchange proved a haven for sophisticated predators to produce and spread deplorable depictions of child sex abuse,' said then assistant attorney-general Brian A Benczkowski of the Justice Department's Criminal Division. 'These sentences affirm that layers of anonymity on the dark web will not prevent the Department of Justice from identifying and holding accountable those who exploit children.'[2] He was echoed by US attorney Don Cochran for the Middle District of Tennessee: 'The sentences imposed on these despicable individuals should ensure that they never have another opportunity to abuse another child. With all that we have, we will continue to hunt down the evil and abominable like-minded individuals who delight in abusing children and bring them to justice.'[3]

But exactly how do you 'hunt down' clever criminals like Faulkner and Falte who practise their particular brand of depravity on the dark web?

Falte created the Giftbox Exchange in 2015 and hid it deep inside the dark web, which meant it could only be accessed by those who sought it out through the anonymous Tor network or another like it. Falte funded the site's operation using bitcoin, the cryptocurrency. And Falte was the site's administrator. He set the membership rules, which in this case – as with most other such groups – meant those wanting to join had to show their commitment by sharing images and footage of pre-teen children being sexually abused. That was the key that opened the door to a network that had more than 72 000 registered users.

The Giftbox Exchange acted like a big, ordered digital library for the licentious and depraved. Postings were categorised by type, including age range, with one labelled 'Babies and Toddlers'. It's hard to type those words. Repeatedly in the research conducted for this book, the question arose of how an individual – let alone 72 000 of them (and some of these clubs have up to two million members) – could be drawn to stealing the innocence of infants and toddlers. That riddle is discussed in Chapter 15, but for now, it's worth reiterating that these people felt protected in large part because of the complex encryption around their online activities. According to the evidence used to prosecute Faulkner, he joined the Giftbox Exchange only weeks after Falte created it and quickly became an administrator. His credentials in this dark space were strong as he had established other sites: a dark web club for sexual predators that hosted more than 200 000 users, and another reserved for producers of child sexual exploitation material.

The powers allocated to Taskforce Argos allow it to act wherever a child victim might be. That's a recognition of two unknowns: because of the nature of this crime, it is often impossible to know the geographic location of the victim until they are found; and secondly, this offence, more than most, occurs seamlessly across international boundaries. With the click of a computer key to perform an upload, predators are able to join an international club that doesn't respect *any* borders: moral, criminal or geographic. And the most effective tool to combat this, according to investigators? It's the covert infiltration of the clubs.

It was Faulkner's – or rather Warhead's – online life that Taskforce Argos operatives took over. US investigators had been able to obtain his passwords shortly after he and Falte were arrested on charges of sexually abusing a young girl. But the passwords merely acted as a key to open the door of the underworld club run by Falte and Faulkner. Now, a senior Argos operative needed to 'become' its chief – he needed to rule the club, without a shred of suspicion being raised that Faulkner was now in custody and his online persona had been taken over by police. Importantly, because club membership dictated that users upload monthly images or videos showing child exploitation – ironically, supposed insurance against law enforcement joining the club and tracking members down – Argos, as in previous operations, needed to play ball. Its rationale was that the images it posted were already in circulation; officers' previous work had brought terabytes of evidence into their inboxes and their uploads were drawn from that – new material was never used. And crucially, it allowed an operative to stay hidden amongst the group's membership and compile evidence that could later be presented to court.

This wasn't new territory, but method acting is not in the skill set of all police officers either. In this case, Paul Griffiths at one point had only seventy-two hours to learn how to deliver an Academy Award–winning performance of Warhead, the senior predator of a global child sex exploitation racket. His language, his choice of words, and the pace of his speech had to match that of Faulkner's, as did the schedule under which he would join conversations and the form of the messages he would post. The challenges were clear. Faulkner was in his late twenties, while Griffiths, a seasoned investigator, was older. Faulkner was Canadian, while Griffiths was from the United Kingdom.

But if it was a numbers game, Griffiths certainly pulled it off. Taskforce Argos slammed the door on the Child's Play club it had taken over in September 2017. By the time Operation Artemis ended, after coverts inside Taskforce Argos had play-acted Warhead for almost a year, a case had been built up against ninety targets on serious charges, and nearly a hundred other users had been tagged because they had produced or possessed child sex material.

Rarely does any investigation run smoothly, and Rouse admits that his covert operators have been caught out on occasion. That's because some administrators tell their lieutenants that if they ever have cause to doubt their credibility, they should ask a specific prearranged question. A couple of times, covert operators faced questions from suspicious members and were stumped. But it was another problem that Rouse and Griffiths ran into with Operation Artemis, an issue they believe carried the risk of bringing down the entire operation – including, according to Rouse, the rescue of children.

An internet security expert working with a journalist from a Norwegian newspaper, *Verdens Gang* or *VG* for short, stumbled across the operation while investigating online child sex exploitation, and the IP address directed them to Sydney. There, the pair visited the offices of the web host, where they were told the registration details. 'A few keystrokes later, we have an answer: the server is leased by Task Force [sic] Argos in Brisbane,' *VG* later explained.[4] Rouse says this isn't true. The server was leased by a backstopped fake identity, with a reference back to Queensland Police. Nonetheless, the Norwegian journalist then contacted Taskforce Argos and asked to meet up.

Rouse acquiesced and organised a meeting at a busy Brisbane CBD eatery.

The journalist wanted an in – an explanation of why local law enforcement was running an online paedophile racket. As a journalist, that seems to me a fair request. But Rouse, who met the journalist while accompanied by Griffiths, didn't want to say a word: 'I knew exactly what he wanted. I was going to the noisiest place I could find in case we were being recorded.' Rouse says he needed to keep the operation active. Taskforce Argos was making significant inroads, demonstrated by children being saved and arrests being made in Europe and the United States. He was miffed that he was being put in a position where his next move had to be dictated by the need to protect his covert officer and keep the operation going. 'One mistake can prove very costly,' Rouse says. That meant bargaining with a journalist he didn't know, from the other side of the world. He laments the media and public understanding around predators, which flies in the face of the fact that more than half of abusers are known to the victim in some way. 'They all want Dennis Ferguson,' he says, referring to the convicted Australian paedophile who stood out through his dress and mannerisms. 'They want the guy in the black raincoat or the white van that pulls up. That's not the truth.'

Rouse agreed to supply *VG* with details of Operation Artemis after they'd swept up as much evidence as possible. 'We had to bargain with them to do that,' he says. There is a flash of anger. 'We wanted to save children.'

•

Rouse dismisses the controversy around the use of undercover operatives, saying his job is both to ensure they work within the letter of the law, and they use the unique skills they have to catch as many predators and to save as many children as possible. Operatives in some cases have to play both sex offenders and teen girls in a bid to catch their prey. Rouse says that acting as a sex offender, to the point where paedophiles believe you are one of them, is a much bigger psychological challenge: 'You are assuming the identity of everything that you exist to end.' He did it as a young officer, knowing his target was an Australian man who had joined his female partner in abusing their daughter. The predator would explain to Rouse, the actor, that the abuse would unfold in the shower, and he liked going into minute detail. 'And my job, to save that girl, was to convince him that I was really interested in that, and then to share stories.' Rouse stops – his own daughter was around the same age.

The role of an undercover child sex crime operative is in a different category from those who go undercover on the streets. Covert workers in drug rings and organised crime empires face physical risk every day. That threat doesn't exist for covert officers online, but the psychological impact is almost impossible to fathom. Arnold Bell, who worked for the FBI for decades, says: 'I've worked murders, rapes, all sorts of stuff. The worst offences, I've seen them.' But child sex crime covert workers such as those he ran in the FBI were a different breed from those who pretended to fit into a gang or a drug deal. 'Somehow,' he says, 'they can block out some of the imagery that they're seeing and can kind of put together the background pieces and identify locations and accents and that kind of stuff.' He knows, despite picking up a wall of awards for saving children, that he couldn't do that. 'I can't have a conversation with a child predator because I want to just reach through and strangle them, and it comes through ...'

Bell says it isn't possible to calculate the worth of a covert officer. In his experience, it is the most effective, and often the only, way to get the required evidence. 'I can go and grab a particular individual for a particular crime, but unless that person talks to me, it stops right there,' he says. Undercover work delivers the pieces that complete the puzzle. A stellar example is the arrest and conviction of Brett Peter Cowan, the serial paedophile with a long history of abusing children, on charges relating to the disappearance of Daniel Morcombe in the lead-up to Christmas 2003. Those charges included murder, indecent treatment of a child and interfering with a corpse. As detailed in Chapter 5, Cowan was brought to justice with the help of a covert police operation staged eight years later. It included an officer posing as a crime boss. His name was 'Paul Fitzsimmons' or 'Fitzy', and he worked to gain Cowan's trust because, in the absence of any evidence, police needed a confession. It took four months, but the effort led to Cowan revealing his involvement – which was captured on camera.

Bob Atkinson was the Queensland police commissioner from 2000 until 2012, which covered the entire period from Daniel's disappearance to Cowan's arrest. Atkinson, who Bell lauds as one of the best leaders the FBI worked with, was involved in more child sex cases in his 44-year police career than he can remember. And he rates the Morcombe case as 'the finest piece of investigation' in terms of a covert operation during those decades. 'Cowan would never have admitted that to someone else,' he says.

Jim Cole, who worked for the US Department of Home Security, jointly ran the Warhead operation with Rouse. He also bristles at criticism over the use of covert operatives. 'The things we did to level the playing field even a little bit were extremely minor compared to what the offenders are doing day in and day out on these platforms around the world,' he says. 'The bad guys aren't constrained by really anything. They're not constrained by policies, are not constrained by law. They're not constrained by jurisdictional boundaries. They don't give a crap about lines on a map.' Legal covert operations provide a 'unique capability' to nab those who are abusing children, Cole says.

Lianna McDonald of Canada's C3P says the public has a weak understanding of how crucial covert work is. 'This isn't like we're dealing with fraud or a widget, and I'm not minimising other types of crime,' she says. But timing is critical in the rescue of children, she explains, 'And there isn't really a playbook on that because in our space, you're dealing with imminent potential danger of children. It's also what we don't know – it's the access to other children [who] offenders may not even be talking about on the dark web.'

'Almost every single case we do, big operations, takes years,' Rouse says. It's not like a 'sausage factory' where a tip inevitably leads to a warrant and then an arrest. The way to save children is by gathering proof they are being abused. Information – passwords and tip-offs and account takeovers – are the key to opening that door. But that means they still need to find the victim and pin down the culprit. They need to download the images and photograph the conversations. That's what is needed in court to give voice to the young child who is being abused. It's a long game, where the passion to make a difference can run up against finite funding and resources. Which makes Taskforce Argos's most successful operation to date, discussed in the next chapter, and which has been running for more than a decade, even more remarkable.

12

Nowhere to hide

The proof is always in the numbers, and on any measure it is Operation Open House that heads the Argos scoreboard. So far it's been going for more than a decade, which underlines how child sex abuse online has spread across the globe, finding a home in as many impoverished countries as in nooks and crannies on the dark web. The effort has resulted in thousands of arrests in numerous countries, but it doesn't make headlines – it's now just part of the core business of those fighting online predators. What's most significant, though, is that the number of children who have been rescued runs into the hundreds, possibly the thousands.

The clues that sustain this operation appear in plain sight – in family social media posts, on sports club bulletin boards, or just about anywhere on the open web that features children. Privacy prohibits this making the news as well. To help an abused child have a fighting chance of rebuilding their life, and their trust in adults, many countries' justice systems preach the importance of anonymity. So far, it is known that 2194 search warrants have been executed and 1660 people have been arrested globally during Operation Open House. Investigators have netted 923 contact offenders: those who become hands-on abusers, raping and sexually assaulting children. In the same period, 873 child victims have been identified. 'That's the stats, and there's nothing that we have ever done that touches that operation,' says Jon Rouse.

Operation Open House, headquartered in Australia, has seen children saved from family homes in the middle of the night, while others have been plucked from hotel rooms, or predators' homes or airport queues. Some of those have been directed to state care, and others now live with extended families. Their ages range from tiny infants to those on the brink of adulthood. Still, investigators increasingly are becoming worried about how this nefarious industry keeps finding new ways to target children, new ways to lure members who want to crow about their exploitative feats, and new ways to combat transparency. Of most concern is that investigators are seeing a 63 per cent contact-offender rate in those apprehended because of their online activities.[1] That means online investigations are pointing at hands-on abusers in three out of every five cases – predators raping and sexually assaulting children before moving the images and footages online to share over and over again. Experts believe the cross-over rate between those offending online and offline sits at around 80 per cent, something we'll explore a bit later. But this figure is also significant because it is being translated into outcomes, with predators being pegged for both as a result of police work. 'The statistics are way above anything else we've ever done, which is why we've done it for nearly eleven years,' Rouse says. The successes go even beyond that, with 98.97 per cent of the searches of premises conducted finding child exploitation material, and 86.6 per cent of suspects found with similar material.[2]

It's worth pausing here to emphasise the unrelenting exploitation faced by a victim whose sexual abuse has been showcased on the dark web. NCMEC President and CEO Michelle DeLaune provided an insight into this when she addressed a US Senate Committee on the Judiciary, in February 2023.[3] She said that child sex abuse images could 'recirculate at disturbingly high rates as increasing numbers of offenders around the world seek out and trade a victim's imagery year after year'. She also provided examples of the utter ongoing horror confronting someone whose abuse is displayed online. In one case, more than 1.19 million graphic sex abuse images and videos involving a female toddler were found in content taken from almost 13 000 offenders. In another, 1.15 million images of a child who was aged between five and nine years old were seen in content seized from more than 21 500 offenders. That recirculation, said DeLaune, carried the risk of great psychological and physical harm for the victims. This cycle of horror can continue even once a victim has left their youth behind, and perhaps had children of their own.

Investigators say that if you were to close your eyes and pin a thumbnail onto a map of the world, the location you've marked will be linked to some inquiry, some liaison or some discussions relating to Operation Open House. So how does it differ from the other operations outlined in previous chapters? In short, many of them have been staged deep inside the internet, a realm characterised by lawlessness. Not so with Operation Open House, where the wrongdoing is not always hidden – and this is what should worry parents and the community at large.

•

The predators we are talking about here are not acting behind closed doors, seeking permission to join clubs where child sex abuse is the currency. Rather, just as this abuse has travelled from the dark room to the dark web, it's now popping up under the same cloak of respectability worn by its users. It's out in the open in innocuous comments added to social media postings. It's lurking publicly in clubs, under the pretence of someone being interested in running or photography or travel. It might be a single comment about the sun-kissed skin of a toddler on the beach, or the legs of a child taking part in a community fun run. It might be a remark posted on a photography site, or in the long list of reviews of a particular tourism site. But there will be something about it that, to the trained eyes of investigators, raises an alert. They may all look harmless, the millions of comments on open sites. But some lead down a dark path.

It is painstakingly slow work for investigators to follow these paths, but there can be gigantic daily wins in terms of arrests and rescues. It sounds like low-hanging fruit – a small transgression here, another there – but don't say that to Rouse, who believes that no fruit hangs low. Every clue has to be triaged because in the past, one brief comment by one person has delivered unimaginable caches of child sex abuse. And if you look at the resources plugged into dark web investigations that can take months and assess 'bang for buck in terms of arrests and children rescued', then as Rouse puts it, Operation Open House is the winner.

Rouse is guarded when talking about Operation Open House because this investigation is not for public consumption. Investigators need to keep some things secret, so they can pounce when predators least expect it. Of course, victim identification remains the key ingredient in the broader toolkit – the ability to track down those being abused from the smallest of hints, then take them to safety. But the young victims rarely put their hands up and lodge a complaint. Often, as discussed earlier, they are frightened, fearing the adult they have learned to love will be taken away if they reveal what has been going on. Or they don't know who to trust. Or they simply have been groomed from the time they could walk and know no better. That means the focus has to be on the predator, whose slip-ups will lead investigators to victims with unrelenting speed.

While he won't talk about the modus operandi or methods here, Rouse does say that Operation Open House was coordinated in response to predators disrupting their own dark arts practices. It became incumbent on investigators to not just match but outwit them at their own terrible game. Then again, while policing has changed a great deal over the years, many methods remain the same. Tracking down peer-to-peer networks where child sex abuse material is being shared will always be part of an investigator's work log. Similarly, infiltrating hidden groups on the dark web allows law enforcement to close big criminal empires protected by rules and regulations, and sometimes sheltering hundreds of thousands of users. And a big chunk of the work taken on by paedophile hunters involves running down tips that come in – via NCMEC, for example – filled with information that will prompt the execution of a search warrant.

However, all of these investigative routes are largely reactive. What about being proactive? How do investigators hunt down predators who are not the subject of tip-offs or undercover deep dives, but who have found new ways to source young children?

The answer to that lies in monitoring the open web, that part of the internet used by families, children and students to post chatter about barbecues in a park or a day at the beach, or to swap recipes or photographic tips, or to seek out recommendations for the next family holiday. This is where most of our online communication occurs, on sites where we are seeking out those with similar interests or posting happy snaps for friends and acquaintances to see. These sites are all legal, and might be run by a school sports administrator or a volunteer group, a parent who sets up the local neighbourhood watch group, or a community organisation planning a photographic exhibition. They cover all interests, from fast cars and fashion to sports, music, camping and stamp collecting. None of the administrators want – or will countenance – criminal activity flourishing under their watch. But predators are always on the lookout for content that will provide access to children, which is the entry ticket for their sordid online activities.

Public sites are usually brimming with information, stories and images involving children, many uploaded by parents driven by pride in their offspring. But who are those posting comments on these sites? What is their interest? Do we know them all? Are parents and administrators aware of the dangers that might be lurking in open social media pages? It's an important question because those pages are becoming the new hunting ground for those with a criminal interest in our children. Investigators are now looking at what might be suspicious on them – in addition to responding to the mountain of information being swapped on the dark web, or being delivered via tips from the public or other law enforcement agencies.

It's a trained eye that might pick up a post suggesting more than the literal meaning of the written words, rather than something overtly suspicious that moderators will move swiftly to remove. This open web focus looks at comments that are not illegal, but perhaps might be a bit odd. Such as a post commenting on the healthy body of a young boy, just out of nappies, playing on the beach. Or a post on the photograph taken of a young girl at a sports carnival. The approach lifts the lid on nuance to find out what might be lurking below. Sometimes, though, the comments carry an almighty big red flag. Let's take the example of a comment about a young boy authored on a computer in the United States: 'He was even hotter two years before this picture.' The commenter has followed the imagery relating to this young boy over a two-year period, all the while considering him 'hot'. Is that a silly comment? A drunken post? Or an indication that this author is on the lookout for others like that boy? In this case, it was the latter, a further post making that clear: 'Check out my profile and add me to Messenger if you like little boys. I have tons of pics to trade.' A calling card, but one that might not always rise to the top of the complaints file. For this type of predator, investigators need to go looking.

The girth of the web is immense and it's impossible to monitor every comment on every public site. This is the problem facing law enforcement, one that highlights the difficult decision about where to place resources. Remember that in 2022, NCMEC received thirty-two million reports of suspicious activity from all around the world. So where does a unit like Taskforce Argos even start? It relies in large part on covert operatives who are able to engage the person making the comments in the hope of obtaining evidence, especially images and film, that will later lead to a conviction.

•

Rouse doesn't like the phrase 'child sex tourism', but it's the language the public understands and it is fertile ground in a probe such as Operation Open House that focuses on the open web, where travelling child sex offenders plan their trips. It's also how many offenders seek out opportunities for accessing young children. Impoverished nations feature highly, with most estimates suggesting several million children worldwide are part of the multibillion-dollar child sex tourism industry. Internet access has simply helped ease the path for many of these sex crime travellers. But it's a difficult area to police because of differing laws and even varying levels of acceptance in different countries. It's an almighty task for investigators: the tsunami of material to investigate; posts that, on the surface, seem innocuous but raise concerns;

a myriad of cultures and laws across the globe; and the limits on law enforcement resources.

'I'm going to show you a photograph,' Rouse says, producing an image of three young Indonesian girls playing by themselves on a sofa. The photograph, to my untrained eye, raises no suspicions. A closer look at Rouse's prompting reveals that the sofa is part of a hotel room, but still, that hardly breeds concern. 'So what are these three girls doing in a hotel room?' Rouse asks. 'And why are they posing in front of a camera?' To me, it still all appears fairly innocent. But a covert operative, having come across this image, will go through bulletin boards and open web conversations to see if they can uncover something that might throw more light on these three girls, and who might be acting as the camera operator. This is a different skill for an undercover agent used to traversing the dark web. Here, there's no dark web to infiltrate and no need to gain the trust of a group of wrongdoers. They're not even following a money trail. Success here comes from sparking a conversation, often one-off engagements where the offender shares details that then lead to an arrest.

Rouse pulls out another photograph. This one is of a middle-aged man sitting on a Santa chair, with three girls to one side of him and another three girls on the other side. The photograph was hidden, but not well, and those who know where to look found it quickly. It was found amongst a cache of others that appeared to show regular contact with children, and four albums focused on a twelve-year-old girl and two nine-year-olds. A covert went on to befriend the man, who, with encouragement, big-noted himself. This is a common trait in paedophiles. They either seem to be lonely or they just love accolades bestowed on them by others – these build them up, make them feel important, respected even. That's why in the dark web, the senior positions – which often involve the worst offences – are so coveted. On this occasion, within a few unguarded chats, the suspect talked about ten-year-olds 'having a crush on him'. His disclosures kept flowing. He'd been in the Philippines for almost six years and his girls were his wife's nieces. In fact, he had married a Filipino woman to access children. 'We took them in to our family six years ago,' he said. 'Touching, playing, blow jobs and ... all that is okay as far as I'm concerned. Once you start it's impossible to stop. I know I just keep taking it one step further. And time goes by.'[4]

That's probably as hard to read as it was to write. But this is what is playing out every day, particularly in countries where transgressions are often overlooked – sometimes because there's a low-level appetite for this behaviour, and sometimes because these relationships deliver food onto the family table.

The covert asked if he could stay with the suspect if he visited the Philippines. The middle-aged man responded by saying it would be difficult. His wife and he were in one room, a second room was for 'my girls', a third was the helper's bedroom and a fourth was for his wife's mother. But he wished the covert luck in his own pursuits.

'I do love the Philippines,' the man said in another missive. 'Young girls are not easy to find unless you marry a Filipino that has one or two and will go along with it. My wife knows that I sometimes play with them, but not as much as I really do or how far I have gone with them.'

The covert operative knew investigators now had a case. They'd captured all the evidence required to arrest, charge and convict this man, who was masquerading as a father. The file was wrapped up and sent to the authorities in the Philippines. Then it just gathered dust. That could have been for a myriad reasons: time, resources, priorities. But the result was the same: inaction. It was only later, after the man had been found to be a US citizen and American authorities had stepped in, that he was extradited to his homeland to face legal consequences.

Such inaction on investigative findings, and the consequential risks that children in danger face, plays on the mind of officers. In some cases, they never hear what happens once they've alerted another country's authorities to wrongdoing. 'You've got these challenging problems on the ground in some of these countries where we've got our standards and our view and our laws and our morals and everything else,' Rouse says. 'But that doesn't always translate in other countries. There's some countries where we will not send a lead because they might execute the offender. In some cases, they might execute the victim. You've got this disparity across the world, and we can only work with the agencies that will work with us.'

It's also a call-out to parents to ensure their own and their children's social media involvement is subjected to the highest possible safety standards. One statistic keeps coming back to me, one I shared earlier: that in 63 per cent of cases, there is evidence that those apprehended are also contact offenders, meaning they have assaulted a child offline. Paul Griffiths says some parents can be 'a little blind to what other people are using images for', adding that 'the amount of those images that appear in an offender's collection is quite frightening'. He says a cache of photographs of children at the beach in swimwear, or in a playground, does not necessarily set off a red alert. But what if they are not the children of the person who filed them away? What if he shouldn't have those photographs in his collection? Griffiths says it's unrealistic for people to stop sharing photographs of their children – almost all of us do it. But his advice is this: 'Just think before you do anything. Do you really need to share that image? Do you really need to share so many images? Is it worth the risk?'

Rouse says: 'The plethora of photographs I've seen of innocent children who have got nothing to do with the person who took the photograph is voluminous.' He also says that Operation Open House, which focuses on the danger behind innocuous public social media postings, is 'the best piece of work we've ever done'. For a taskforce globally lauded for its work in this area, this is a big call. And it's one we should all heed.

13

Follow the money

In 2020, a trickle that became a stream of tiny financial transactions to fund child sexual abuse, eventually became a flood that destroyed some of Australia's biggest business reputations. And it had the unintended, but enduringly good, impact of adding a valuable weapon to the armoury for the fight against child exploitation. At the heart of the flood was the detective work of the Australian Transaction Reports and Analysis Centre (AUSTRAC), the federal government agency charged with monitoring the legality of money flowing in and out of the country. Its main target was Westpac, one of the Big Four banks that dominate the Australian share market and the nation's commerce. AUSTRAC swamped Westpac's reputation with a civil court action, alleging negligence in discerning and reporting large-scale money laundering between 2012 and 2019. It accused the bank of breaching anti-money laundering and counterterrorism financing laws on more than twenty-three million occasions, involving $11 billion in transactions. Westpac was duly ordered by the court to pay the highest civil penalty in Australian history: $1.3 billion.[1]

Some of Westpac's failings involved suspicious transactions related to child exploitation in the Philippines, including two associated with child sex offenders. While AUSTRAC's allegations covered much broader ground than child exploitation, it was that revelation that tore at the heart of the bank's integrity, and fuelled the public's displeasure. Westpac, Australia's oldest bank, was shaken. Its share price was ravaged and its leadership team became the target of angry investors and an indignant public – CEO Brian Hartzer, along with other executives, resigned.[2]

The accusations centred on claims that payments by hundreds of customers showed telltale connections to child abuse not just in the Philippines but other countries, too – the bank later confirmed this was so. Many of the amounts, in isolation, were tiny, but they were frequent and they met the red flags AUSTRAC had given all financial institutions at the start of the 2010s, when it asked them to be alert to the misuse of their services by child sex abusers. That included regular, small transactions involving countries seen to be the source of exploitative material, particularly if the customer had no identifiable family link with such a nation. But Westpac took until 2018 to pay attention.

The action by AUSTRAC not only put the spotlight on Westpac but also on the business side of child sexual exploitation, which, thanks to the ubiquity of the internet and the ever-present desire to profit from it, was burgeoning. A shamed Westpac, keen to retrieve its reputation, responded by both reforming its own business practices and by funding an initiative designed to stop the future channelling of money from Australian viewers of sexual violence to their evil partners in crime in other countries.

The scale of the business that sits behind child sexual exploitation is difficult to ascertain, but the money can be traced back to two things. One is the willingness of certain people to pay to see exploitative material, principally via pay-per-view or subscription sites – something chronicled in earlier chapters in regard to several operations. The other is the rising trend of sexploitation. The motivation by offenders here, as discussed in Chapter 1, is focused almost exclusively on forcing children to perform sex acts on camera. The target, who is increasingly likely to be a male in his late teens, is subsequently blackmailed to pay for the removal of videoed or photographed sex acts he has been enticed to perform by someone with a fake online persona. In both instances, the money is required to be transmitted to the perpetrator. And this is where ICMEC in Australia has come into its own, working with regulators and financiers to alert them to how to spot these transactions and then report them.

Essentially, ICMEC's work invokes one of the oldest principles adhered to by investigators of wrongdoing: follow the money.

•

Jon Rouse, who is a non-executive director of ICMEC, says 'taking out the consumer base' in commercial online child sex operations is the most effective way of dismantling them. 'There are no low-hanging fruit,' he says. 'We need to chase down every single target we can and that means taking out the people who are paying for it.' The growing and 'horrendous' trend in finance sextortion poses a great challenge to law enforcement, however, because much of it originates in overseas-based scamming, from hoaxes around the death of a distant relative, to the promise of romance. And despite their actions costing Australians millions of dollars, perpetrators – including organised crime groups – often benefit from finite police resources, legislative limits and even regulatory corruption, says Rouse.

Anna Bowden, ICMEC Australia's savvy CEO, says her organisation – now funded by Westpac in the wake of the financial transaction scandal – aims to help banks pick up payments directed at online child sex abuse, including financial sextortion, and then to feed quality information to AUSTRAC and law enforcement agencies. Bowden says members of a working group made up of law enforcement, bank and not-for-profit representatives who have access to huge reserves of online data, collaborate to finger transactions that might otherwise escape attention. 'Sitting in a financial crime unit seeing $30 being paid for school fees [to an overseas destination] doesn't mean anything by itself,' she says. But in tandem with other information or data, a case might be built to show that transaction is funding online child sex pursuits. This approach would almost certainly have highlighted the payments that dented Westpac's reputation only a few years ago. Bowden says the earlier environment, in which banks were acting from a place of compliance or risk mitigation, has now flipped with acknowledgement of the size of the problem: 'It's fully turned. The banks show up, they share information. They're not able to share data with each other, but they'll certainly share information and what they are seeing, and they'll do it totally off their own bat.' Many bankers, once they are made aware of the scale of the child sex abuse scourge, are also offering to volunteer on weekends. Bowden says: 'They're actually leaning in now and saying, "We want to help because I've got two young kids and I don't want to see this happen. What can I do to help?"'

While online child abuse is itself often not driven by money, more and more financial crime networks are emerging that have the ability to produce content and then distribute and sell it. 'It's much easier to get to victims unfortunately. You can go online and find someone very quickly,' Bowden says. The perpetrators include single operators. 'There are dads sitting online at night doing stuff,' explains Bowden. 'But more and more they are networking with each other. And then there's people where it's not necessarily about the content, it's about the profit. So they're organising criminal networks in order to just extort and make money.'

Bowden says following the money is crucial because otherwise, many of these crimes will go unreported. She adds: 'A lot of desperate families will groom their own children or they'll groom people who they know, in poor situations. That then provides content which provides a market for funding. And that's why the money piece is really quite important.'

That issue of non-reporting, particularly by child victims, is easily overlooked. Bowden, herself a victim of child sex abuse, says she couldn't report the horror she suffered, and most children don't. Many also don't understand the extent of the abuse they suffered until they are older, when it might be too late to report it. 'For decades and decades, these offenders continue to abuse children,' says Bowden. 'What we are doing at ICMEC is incredibly powerful because in the absence of that reporting, when people like me as a little child couldn't report it, we're actually digging around on the internet and we're working with the banks to pick up the digital footprint that exists ...' While the end goal remains to save the victims, often the only way to do that is by tracking down the offenders.

The total amount of money being paid to extorters, whose demands can range from $50 to $10000, is difficult to tally because only one in four teens is likely to report the offence. In addition, investigators say the overseas-based sextorters will also negotiate, and perhaps include vouchers which can be transferred into cash online for a small fee. Regardless, this is now considered such a serious threat that, in December 2022, the FBI issued a National Public Safety Alert on Financial Sextortion Schemes.[3] Meanwhile, a global threat assessment by the WeProtect Global Alliance, which involves more than 100 governments, seventy companies and a host of charities, has labelled child sexual exploitation and abuse online as 'one of the most urgent and defining issues of our generation'.[4]

In case you think this is something that only happens in other countries, consider this: in 2022, more than 500 current Australian bank, financial services and digital accounts were closed down because of a joint AFP and AUSTRAC effort called Operation Huntsman. It prompted the banks to help facilitate the closure of accounts that were held in Australia but linked to international organised crime syndicates. A year later, investigators continue to comb through the details of more than 1000 Australian accounts that have seen money flowing out of the country due to financial sextortion.[5] The ACCCE says it is recording more than 100 reports of this type of sextortion each month, and more than 90 per cent of victims are male, usually aged between fifteen and seventeen – although some are as young as ten. Julie Inman Grant, Australia's eSafety Commissioner, is seeing a similar pattern, but with young men up to twenty-four years of age being targeted. 'It's very lucrative,' she says. 'We've had very distressed young people coming to us who have already given up about $10 000.' Some had negotiated the payment down to $150, but once the criminals 'got the $150, they knew they could access money and kept coming back to them'. While doing this research, I was also told of suicides in Australia that had followed the sextortion of teen boys.

Males and females are being targeted differently, too. Boys are being sextorted for money, while more intimate imagery or an escalation in sexual activity is more likely to be demanded of girls. AFP Assistant Commissioner Hilda Sirec says boys seem to be 'more persuaded with the quick hit' conducted by offshore syndicates. In other words, they have the characteristics most global businesses seek in their 'customers' – they are a ready and vulnerable market. 'When you've got a gorgeous young lady between fourteen and seventeen prepared to send you some intimate images, the boys are turning around and saying, "Yep, giddy up on. I'm in for this."'

NCMEC, the child protection organisation that Michelle DeLaune heads in the United States, benefits from the fact that tech companies are required under US law to provide information to it about any suspicious online activity. NCMEC then provides that information to authorities in countless countries, including Australia. 'If they see something works, then they're going to double down and keep going after that pool,' says DeLaune about what motivates these offenders. Inman Grant says, 'This is global organised crime,' adding that many tips have zeroed in on the West African nations of Nigeria, Ghana and Côte d'Ivoire, and more recently on the Philippines and India. The roots of this illegal phenomenon in Australia can be traced back to the proliferation of email scams a few years ago, where recipients were told that compromising photographs of them existed and they urgently needed to transfer money or risk having the images exposed online. I remember receiving one of these messages, and promptly binned it. But Inman Grant says that in 2020, perpetrators deliberately targeted international full-fee-paying students who might not have understood the Australian dating lexicon. 'That's how it started,' Inman Grant says.

The target now is young men, and this is creating pots of gold for overseas-based organised crime networks. DeLaune says both the 'lone wolf' predators and the crime networks play on boys' embarrassment, shame and guilt, and their modus operandi is polished. 'There has been some evidence of that when the criminals have somebody on the hook, then there might be a new person who then takes over the chat,' she says. That person may, for example, speak better English or be better able to extort the funds from a vulnerable teenager in another country. The pattern and execution seen in this crime poses a 'unique threat to children', DeLaune told a US Senate

Committee on the Judiciary in 2023.[6] 'Offenders will use fake accounts and stolen online profile photos to pose as a young female and target teenage boys to convince them to produce a nude or sexually explicit image,' said DeLaune. 'Almost immediately after obtaining an image, the offender will demand payment through gift cards or a peer-to-peer electronic payment system and will threaten to release the child's image if payment is not received.' It can happen with lightning speed, sometimes in minutes, and the outcome can be tragic. 'NCMEC is aware of over a dozen instances since 2021 in which a teenage boy has taken his life as a result of being victimised by financial sextortion,' said DeLaune.

While the crime is relatively new, it is one of the most rapidly evolving online sex exploitation crimes against children that DeLaune has witnessed in thirty years. And while reporting rates are low, DeLaune says those reports where girls are victims are usually lodged by a friend, family member or a parent. In the case of boys, when it is reported, it is usually the victim who lodges a complaint. The swift emergence of this issue is very alarming, DeLaune says, and most of the reported cases had occurred on four platforms: Instagram, Snapchat, Facebook and Google Hangouts.

•

Just as dark rooms gave way to the dark web, and as a result investigators have had to disrupt the way they police crime, the concept of organised crime has changed over the last century. It was the bankers, lawyers and businessmen who set up the Chicago Crime Commission in 1919 who first used the term 'organised crime' to describe 'professional criminals'. Then, during the Great Depression, organised crime largely referred to gangsters and racketeers who organised themselves into gangs and syndicates. The Mafia owned the term from the 1950s. But what does it really mean?

'It is clear that the concept of organised crime has expanded beyond highly structured and hierarchical organisations to encompass less-formal groups and undefined criminal networks,' reported Queensland's Organised Crime Commission of Inquiry in 2015.[7] The inquiry went on to say that the 'virtual criminal underworld' was full of individual 'criminal entrepreneurs' who shared their 'knowledge, experience, expertise and, importantly, their vile and abusive product in a "crime-as-a-service" business model'. This is what the pay-per-view model of online child sex crime looks like. It's what the subscription sites, which host gut-wrenching abuse, look like. It's what the secret dark web paedophile sites, with their organised structures, strict hierarchies and savage security, look like. It can be seen in this message from the Australian head of one of those dark web paedophile clubs to his members: 'Thanks for another hard yet successful year. We do something that thousands rely on and visit almost daily. And we do it with a risk to our own lives and while hiding from the law. This is a huge undertaking and something that most others do only for reward.' Sextorters are merely the most recent organised crime group.

The Organised Crime Commission also found that, while there were many examples of lone offenders, there were 'disturbing instances of huge rings of offenders' involved in sextortion. Interpol described 'call centre-style offices staffed by cyber-blackmail agents who are provided with training and offered bonus incentives such as holidays, cash or mobile phones for reaching financial targets'.[8] In addition to picking individual targets, the criminals were also targeting dating websites, chat rooms and social networking platforms. One global syndicate that operated out of the Philippines was described as 'massive'. An investigation coordinated by Interpol led to the identification of up to 195 people who were working for organised crime groups connected with that syndicate, and resulted in fifty-eight arrests.[9] Victims were found in many countries, including Australia. One seventeen-year-old, who had sent explicit images of himself to a person he thought was a teen girl, took his own life.

Lianna McDonald of C3P says the 'extreme organisation' behind the abuse keeps her awake at night, with multiple offenders 'working in concert to abuse one or more children'. She also says that 'children are moved amongst offender communities. We have a lot of extreme sadistic, physical, psychological and emotional damage being done.' McDonald says the offender community has become 'far more emboldened and more organised amongst themselves' and now shares capacity, tactics and a new sense of camaraderie, and provides 'encouragement to young new people coming into the fold'. McDonald warns: 'There's really just this unregulated no-man's lawless land. I don't think we have actually seen yet the [true] level of depravity and we're not even close to being under the hood on this mess.'

Investigators believe these syndicates use a strategy whereby large numbers of potential offenders attempt to make contact with children. They have a methodology, akin to a script, and work out of pop-up-type call centres, equipped with quotas and targets. Investigators also believe they use hierarchical structures and rely on systematic funnelling to move money from their teen victims into Australian bank accounts, before the cash is then moved offshore. Because a syndicate in Africa or Asia cannot open an Australian bank account, 'money mules' – who may or may not be aware of the criminality behind what they are doing – are used to open accounts. Some teens who are not able to pay the ransom to keep their sex acts from being distributed online are also being forced to open accounts, and given instructions of where to then send the money deposited in them. This is where the AFP and AUSTRAC, through Operation Huntsman, have focused their attention: tracking down the money being siphoned to offshore accounts. 'Huntsman is our primary disruption activity,' says Hilda Sirec, the aim being to ensure the criminal enterprise doesn't grow, pushing Australia to become a 'middle criminal pathway'. Sirec says, 'We've got to cut that off.'

Whatever commercial enterprise criminals are waging, whether it's online in dark web clubs or by sextorting our teens, there is a gluttonous demand to procure children to produce new content. And the news is unlikely to get better into the future. Dr Rick Brown of the Australian Institute of Criminology, who wrote *Eliminating Online Child Sexual Abuse Material*, warns of the danger that the hidden markets will grow in size 'because people find it easier to move into the dark net space'. He adds: 'So the potential for that to grow as a criminal market is something significant.' A wealth of opportunities also exists for organised crime networks. Sextorting money off teenagers is just the newest type of crime being capitalised on by those same networks who introduced scams promising anyone who would listen a life of wealth and love.

Investigation expert Warren Bulmer says sextortion is definitely organised crime. It's simply that the criminals' 'shtick is fraud'. And, he says, 'they are very good at capitalising on the latest trending issue, and turning that into a fraud'. He's right. Just consider the meteoric increase in scams not just around lotteries and romance but COVID vaccines, for example, or on the back of the heartache in Ukraine or the National Disability Insurance Scheme. 'Just pick a topical issue where they can get the most victims, and they'll turn that into a scam,' says Bulmer.

Australians lost more than $851 million to scams in 2020, a record amount.[10] But the cost is so much higher when you include the heartache, mental health challenges and suicides of our children. Michelle DeLaune says threats will continue to emerge. For example, in the four years to 2022, NCMEC saw a 567 per cent increase in reports relating to the 'sexual enticement of a child'. The COVID-19 pandemic was a factor here, with a distinct increase in the number of young girls being targeted. In fact, DeLaune's team tracked predators talking openly in the dark web about how easy it was to find children during the pandemic. The comments included: 'How many single or divorced dads are now stuck at home with their horny daughters that can't visit their boyfriends? That must create some opportunities lol.' And: 'I hope there are terabytes of new content being created right now with bored dads and older brothers stuck at home all day with their kids/ siblings.'

Online child sex victim identification expert Paul Griffiths says the changing modus operandi of predators challenges investigators because it requires a different mindset to tackle. He says 'it's worrying on two fronts because you've got the straight financial aspects of the crime, and then the lasting damage to the kids as well. Some of the intricacies of the way that the exploitation is actually being applied is forcing the kids to commit acts that they wouldn't have otherwise committed – because [the predators] know they have more financial value once they've done that.'

'We need to track down every single target,' says Rouse, meaning the criminals who sexually assault young children, those who upload harrowing images, the customers of pay-per-view and subscription operations, members of the huge dark web operations that harbour offenders, and those who have 'zero sexual interest in kids but who just want money'. And that's because at the centre of all those networked predator streams are children.

Part 5

Abused and abuser

14

Innocence stolen

Casey is walking home from school, in a little town on the other side of the world from Australia, when she is intercepted and taken to safety by police. Paul Griffiths is in her home along with other investigators, searching for the evidence that will send her attacker to jail. Later, he will find videos of Casey being abused in a room in that home – images of a little girl only just old enough to navigate the path to and from school by herself. Griffiths tells this story to illustrate the relief he felt at not meeting this child who had been so badly exploited.

That response is common amongst investigators. They eschew any opportunity to meet the child they have been instrumental in rescuing. Exceptions exist, of course, with the odd investigator sitting in a lecture theatre to watch a person they helped save graduate from high school, before heading to university with the sordid story of their childhood well behind them. Mike Duffey from the Florida Department of Law Enforcement is one of those. 'When you actually meet the child and you're able to stop [that abuse] from occurring, and then they hug you, it changes your life,' he says. 'It makes you feel like, I'm never going to quit doing this. Never.' But that decision to meet the victim – and in some cases even keep in touch with their family – is rare. Most investigators daily see the turpitude of men who become monsters during wicked crimes that steal the smiles and the futures of the children they hurt. They also see the pain on the innocent faces of their victims, the demeaning acts these children are forced to perform, often by someone they've been told they can trust. Their job is to find the evidence to rescue that child, and that done, they move on. That's the point where most of them want to take a step back. They don't want the child to meet someone who has viewed their private torment.

Online child sex abuse often magnifies and prolongs the awful real-life or contact assault. Once uploaded, it follows a victim for years, decades even, because it can't be pulled back or retrieved. A video shared in a secret online group might be viewed a million times, and every time someone sees it, whether it's a day, week, month or year following the abuse, that child is violated again. Sometimes it's part of a pay-per-view package, or a fresh upload offered to a new group. Regardless, it can be viewed again and again. The impact on a victim is immeasurable because they cannot escape it. They just don't know who has seen them at their most vulnerable.

The original offence, which may have taken place in a bedroom or bathroom or hotel or the back of a car, can forge its own reminders across the life of the victim. The smell of their attacker. The beer he swigged. His cigarettes, or aftershave, or beard. The taste of something that sat uneaten in their own crime scene. A colour. An accent. 'It's like a car accident,' says Bravehearts founder Hetty Johnston. 'Because it is so traumatic, your brain protects you. But it gives you the information back in dribs and drabs, and the same happens a lot of the time with sex offences.'

This is how one victim describes it:

'I still get glimpses. Someone will be talking about something and the pieces just come back in a chaotic order.'

'I may never remember all of the details, and I honestly hope I don't.'

'When it first happened, I thought [I] was going crazy. I was doubting myself. Surely I'm making this up ...'

'I don't remember all the details but lying in bed with him awake and him telling me stuff. I asked my parents and they said it was fine; he was babysitting me.'

The thing with online abuse is that there's a multiplier effect that kicks in. There's a material difference between a one-off dreadful assault and an assault that ends up being replayed on-screen for the world to see, perhaps forever. Of the eighty-five million images, videos and other content reported to NCMEC in 2021, about 26 per cent was unique. That means 74 per cent of the content – almost sixty-three million images – was being continually redistributed online by offenders.[1]

'It is much worse on so many levels. If it is played over and over and over again and people can see it, they even can't walk down the street without thinking people are looking at you.'

'Statistically, if your abuse is shared online you are much less likely to report it; you don't want anyone to know about it.'

Many victims, like the woman quoted here, manage to traverse the rocky path ahead, almost always with significant professional health assistance. They go on to graduate from school and university and have families of their own. But others are locked into unhappiness, unable to escape the sex toys that find their way to them, sent by strangers years after the abuse; or the email or letter from another attacker who has found their address and wants to comment on their 'performance'.

Lianna McDonald from Canada's C3P says she sees many children continue to be stalked online for years after they are abused: 'There are serious, serious safety concerns pertaining to some of this population. And we don't have the resources. We don't have the laws. We don't really know how to deal with it.' The Florida Department of Law Enforcement's Mike Duffey says he, too, has received letters from offenders, who claim they are similar to him – that just as he works to counter child exploitation, their goal is similarly to protect children. 'It's strange,' he says, 'you just try to wrap your head around it but you can't.'

Many victims are diverted from the rosy future promised at birth and find themselves in trouble with the law, or facing significant mental health challenges. In some cases, the anguish is unbearable and they take their own life. 'It's a $64 million question,' Griffiths says, because some children make a 'startling recovery. And I say startling because it just startles me that they can recover from it. Others, who very often probably weren't the victim of anything as severe, can't cope with what's happened.' Research is needed to find the factor that allows some victims to thrive and others not, he says. Hetty Johnston echoes Griffiths' comments: 'Some are very resilient, really strong people, and some are not.' Psychologist Amanda Frame, who has worked as a police officer in a child abuse unit, says she's found reservoirs of resilience in most children: 'So even when adverse things happen in life, as long as they're getting that right support, they have the skills to be able to deal with that adversity.' The age at which children are harmed also plays a part. It can be harder for them once they reach their teenage years, as one victim explains:

'It's not just as a teenager. I still feel really unworthy, all the time. Even with my closest friends, I think it's a chore to hang out with me. The background is I had to pleasure people. It's serving.'

'I hated sleepovers with friends. I would lie on my little mattress on the floor. I felt it wasn't safe to go to sleep. I struggle when I have to stay away now.'

•

Just as there's a multiplier effect from the viewing of exploitation material online, there's a multiplier effect that creates more victims. Those affected by child sex abuse can include the victim's family and friends, their school and extracurricular communities, and even those close to their attacker, who often are forced to confront the fact that their partner or parent – the person they trusted more than anyone else – is a secret child sex abuser.

Hetty Johnston knows all about this. She remembers the day her corporate, scheduled and well-ordered life was reduced to an unruly whirlwind where nothing made sense. A phone call from her husband, Ian, who was holidaying with their daughter in New Zealand, ended the world she knew. He told Hetty how his father had abused their daughter. Johnston still shakes her head at the memory. 'I loved that guy,' she says. 'I thought he was the best thing since sliced bread, you know?' Her father-in-law, who was a serial offender, was sent to jail and has since died. 'It took the rug out from under me,' says Johnston. 'Everything was mobile. I couldn't get a handle on anything, [there was] nothing to hang on to, nothing static. Everything was up in the air; everything was just exploding.' Often, families split at this point, because of the recriminations, blame, disbelief. They all become victims of one person's assault.

Layers of complexity and torment can be added. Let's take the example of where a father is the offender, and the mother believes the abused child instinctively and immediately. 'There are so many women living in cars now because the child told the mother, who stood up to the husband,' Johnston says. She then leaves the family home, taking the children. Johnston continues: 'They've got nowhere to go or they're couch surfing. The kid's whole school life is disrupted.' And the consequence of all that, in

Johnston's twenty-five years of experience? 'The little kid who disclosed is going to think, This is all my fault.'

Let's take another example, where a child makes the disclosure but their mother doesn't believe them. Or possibly she does, but family economics mean she 'chooses' to stay where she is, with a roof over her head. What damage does that do to the family relationship, and to the child who courageously sought help? Between 96 and 98 per cent of disclosures, Johnston says, are found to be accurate. A child rarely lies when it comes to finding their voice and seeking help, and in that case there are lifelong consequences, including for the relationship between the child and the person to whom they disclosed the abuse. Hetty Johnston says we need to listen to our children: 'They might not have all the words, but we need to get on that little chair and understand what they are telling us. We need to listen.'

Former police chief Bob Atkinson remembers as a young detective being told by a fifteen-year-old girl that her father was raping her. The father was arrested and immediately made a full admission. Atkinson took the teen home, expecting her mother to be both traumatised and shocked: 'We sat in the kitchen and the mother looked at her [daughter] across the table, and she said to their own daughter: "So who's going to pay the fucking bills now?"' The mother knew, but chose not to act. 'Maybe she thought that in my world, I'll just put up with it, he's not bothering me. If he's drunk at night, he gets into my daughter's bed,' says Atkinson. He says that taught him that not every child feels they can speak up.

Let's take yet another example, one which easily rivals the first two in the degree of heartbreak. Children don't necessarily have all the words to explain what has happened. A child may believe they've alerted the non-offending parent to what is happening in their bedroom when the lights are turned off – perhaps they have, perhaps they haven't. But even if they have, they can remain stuck in a perilous environment. 'I can't tell you how many of these children I've spoken to over the years,' Johnston says. 'They hate, literally cannot speak to, or will not respond to their parents anymore. They shut them down entirely.'

> 'It strikes me really deep. I was of service to [my mother]. I looked after my younger sibling and cleaned the house. It was a Cinderella tale. I wasn't there as a child. I was there to do stuff.'

> 'My whole family ostracised me when I started asking questions. They cut me off. That's the majority of cases. People don't talk about it for that reason.'

The multiplier effect in the world of victims extends to the effects on friendship groups and classrooms. A child might act up, misbehave, play truant. What happened might stunt their ability to make friends, and certainly to have a partner when they reach their teen years. Studies offer a long list of consequences of child sex abuse, including depression, post-traumatic stress disorder, antisocial behaviours, eating disorders, alcohol and drug misuse, parenting difficulties and poverty. This affects all those around the victim, inside and outside the family, and can continue to do so when the victim is older.

'It's been so hard to have kids. I want them to have grandkids in my life, but a big part of that is I don't know how safe they are. I feel sorry for them. I don't have family support like others. It's the gift that keeps giving.'

'I'm constantly hyper hyper vigilant to the degree it's rationally not good for my kids. I want them to take risks but I don't like them leaving home. I have so much guilt and I don't know what the impact on them will be.'

The impact is incomparable when a life is lost. Carol Todd and Sonya Ryan both know the anguish of losing a child as a result of an online predator. As described in Chapter 1, Carol's fifteen-year-old daughter, Amanda, took her own life, but not before she posted a YouTube video where she used a series of flashcards to tell the story of how she was blackmailed into exposing her breasts on a webcam. 'Amanda's story has fanned out more than locally in my community,' says Carol. 'It's fanned out across the world.' Carol has also met a handful of parents of boys who have died by suicide. 'And I have to say, sadly, when I ask them did they know what sextortion was before this happened to their child, they all said "No".' She says it's part of human nature, perhaps, to not pay attention until something happens close to home, until 'tragedy hits'.

Sonya Ryan's fifteen-year-old daughter, Carly, was murdered by an online predator who groomed Carly to the point she thought they were dating. Sonya's plea comes from terrible experience: 'Create a shield of protection around your child. It's too dangerous to put your child online and let them go. Children don't have life experiences to be able to deal with these type[s] of criminals. Kids think it's never going to happen to them.' Sonya's suffering has seen her devote her life to protecting children, by creating online safety education resources and forcing changes in the law. She knows nothing will bring Carly back, but she's hell-bent on preventing other children from meeting the same end.

Many others can be entrapped in the awful wake of abuse, including the partners and families of the offenders – yet another layer of victims. Natalie Walker knows of many whose marriages have ended after finding their husband engaged in online sex abuse or accessing images on a computer. She was drawn in by news coverage of Operation Auxin (discussed in Chapter 5) when the wife of a perpetrator was named. 'She was not a person of interest,' says Walker. 'She was not a suspect. She had just married someone who had now been charged with child abuse material.' Yet this woman was being shamed and blamed almost as though she had colluded with the abuser, when in fact her whole world had collapsed too.

As related earlier, Operation Auxin had more than 700 Australian targets and they came from all walks of life. 'I knew statistically that around three-quarters of these men would have an intimate partner, and then half of them would have kids,' Walker says. 'And I thought if this was a natural disaster of this size, we would do something for these families.' PartnerSPEAK, an organisation that helps the non-offending partners and families of online child sex abusers, followed. Walker says that non-offending partners are often asked how it was they didn't know. She says what's particularly harrowing about that question is that it's the first question women ask themselves. 'In eighteen years, I've never had someone say, "Oh, once he was charged it all made perfect sense."'

So, in her experience, which now extends over almost twenty years, do the non-offending partners offer up a similar modus operandi or character traits for those who have stolen their trust? Walker says the only common trait she hears about is that the offenders are usually 'experts in stealth'. She says: 'Most of the people who come to us have no idea, and they've been living in the same house, sleeping [in] the same bed, sharing the same computers. And when the knock at the door comes, the vast majority of the time the non-offending partner has no idea at all.' It is often when that knock on the door happens that the non-offending partner will seek out PartnerSPEAK. 'We took ninety-eight calls just in December [2022],' Walker says. A realisation by investigators that families are torn apart by an arrest has also seen Walker train law enforcement in each state. And they are increasingly working together, with police calling PartnerSPEAK as they close warrants.

Investigator Warren Bulmer says most cases still involve an offender who is known to the child. So any arrest will almost always automatically cause disruption in the family. That has a multitude of consequences, from divorce to houses being repossessed and significant mental health challenges. 'So when we go in and rescue a child, it's a happy story ... but we destroy lives when we do it,' Bulmer says. Recently, Natalie Walker attended a suburban home where twelve law enforcement officers were turning the place upside down. It looked ransacked, and the family was in a state of disbelief. 'What are they meant to do?' Walker doesn't expect an answer. The list of victims of an online sex abuse case just keeps getting longer, and that makes the number of victims impossible to gauge.

Clinical and forensic psychologist Dr Michael Bourke says up to 3 per cent of the population have impulses that could lead to a child being sexually assaulted, online or offline. But conviction rates involve only a tiny subset of the offender group because about a dozen hurdles have to be cleared on the way to a verdict. For example, says Bourke, for somebody to be convicted, the child needs to understand that they have been assaulted. If they are too young to understand, someone has to catch the perpetrator during an assault, or find evidence such as an image or footage. 'There's a whole lot of kids who don't even know that something's happened. They were asleep, or pre-verbal, they're infants, or have cognitive delays,' Bourke says. The hurdles only begin there. The victim also needs to be able to communicate what happened, and they have to be believed by someone. That someone needs to be a responsible person, not a seven-year-old peer, who has to then make the decision to call the police. 'So that person can't say, "Well, we're going to handle it within the family", or "We're going to handle it within the church", or "We're going to handle it within the school",' he says.

All those steps have to occur in quick succession so evidence can be collected. Police then have to present sufficient evidence to a prosecutor, who has to ensure specific legal standards are met. Then a trial might occur. But even then, the offender might plead to a lesser offence.

They then have to be found guilty – and lose every appeal they lodge. The truth is that few victims go beyond the first few steps. 'So 84 per cent of victims never disclose what has happened to them,' Bourke says. And that is across the board: online and offline, children and adults. 'So we think it's less than 1 per cent of these men are showing up in our police records with the red dot that says "Be careful of this guy; he is a sex offender",' says Bourke.

•

So where is the voice of the victim in this savage crime? Where is the voice of those who are abused online, over and over, but whose attacker is never charged, or never convicted? Where is the voice of those who, because of what Bourke has explained, never tell anyone of their childhood horror? Judge Salvatore Vasta, who used to prosecute online child sex cases, says he saw it as the missing link in these cases – the 'backstory' of all the victims found in the images presented to the court. 'Who is their voice?' he asks. 'And they are re-victimised every time a paedophile swaps or trades or shares images of them being abused.'

'We don't hear from them enough. We need to be aware that the vast majority don't report it. You don't want the only family you have lashing out at you.'

And that's at the heart of how Rouse is planning to spend the next stage of his working life. At the moment, even in court cases, a defendant is judged on the severity and volume of the images in their collection – in the same way a drug dealer faces charges on the purity and weight of their supply. That's the only way, at the moment, that a court can make sense of the crime. Over time, police investigators have tried to guide that narrative by looking at a defendant's place in a network, the popularity of the platforms they were on, how long they'd been sharing images. 'But that misses one thing,' Rouse says. 'And that's the victim. We're treating those images just like they are drugs, when there is a child who at some point in their life has had a horrendous act captured on video or images taken. That's become a commodity in the child sex offender community. But that child's voice is completely lost in the justice system.' Rouse says the community often hears a judge talk of 'abhorrent behaviour', or that the abuse was not 'a victimless crime'. 'Damn shit it's not,' he says. 'But we're not recognising the victim at all. They don't get a say in it.' And meanwhile, images of them being abused continue to circle the globe.

Rouse and Dr Michael Salter, Scientia Associate Professor of Criminology at the School of Social Sciences at the University of New South Wales (UNSW), are working on an out-of-the-box idea, no less novel than those policing techniques Taskforce Argos has employed over for the past thirty years. Argos has contributed huge volumes of cases to the database held by Interpol. As outlined earlier, they've found images of children who are being abused in the collections of offenders who were arrested. In thousands of cases, those children have been rescued. 'We could find those people, who are now adults,' Rouse says. And that offers hope in two big new areas. The first is research. 'Where are they now? What's happened to them in the past twenty years? Are they dead? In jail? Are they offending?

Are they thriving and doing really well? Why are some thriving and not others?' These are Rouse's questions, not mine, and they could spark research that changes every facet of how victims are supported.

The second area is even more ambitious. The images of those children – twenty years on, fifteen years on, ten years on, five years on – are still racing around the web, being sought by predators, and shared continuously. Online sex abuse is a crime that just doesn't have a full stop. 'Those images continue to circle the globe. We are continuing to find them in collections here in Australia and across Europe and across America,' Rouse says. But what if investigators tracked down those victims and offered them the opportunity to detail the impact the abuse has had on them? Yes, those would be hard conversations, but if the victim could provide a video impact statement, it could be saved. And then, says Rouse, 'every time an investigator makes another arrest and triages another hard drive against our AVID, they will get an alert that a victim impact statement is available from the child depicted in the image'.

Salter, an expert in child sexual exploitation, says 410 Australian victims are registered on the Interpol database, and sexual abuse images of many of them remain highly traded online. Overseas research by Salter indicates that some victim survivors are looking for their own abuse images online, and then reporting them and seeking their removal. 'If they don't do that,' he says, 'then there's actually nobody who's proactively seeking the removal of their material, so their material is just shared really widely online.' Significant safety implications sit alongside this: survivors are being recognised face-to-face by predators; offenders are using the content to blackmail victim survivors; and victims are routinely being identified by the offender community, and their details widely shared. 'That becomes an immediate safety risk for that person, their family and children,' Salter says. Other countries are endeavouring to act on behalf of victims, and that's what Rouse and Salter are advocating in Australia. For example, in the United States, victims are notified when a seizure is made that includes images of them, and that has allowed civil suits where offenders can be sued for emotional damage. 'We have nothing like that in Australia,' Salter says.

Currently, court discussions in this country merely circle around the number of images and where they were found and how they were viewed. But what about the ongoing heartache of the person who features in them? Salter says judges and juries cannot understand the impact of victims' sexual abuse being viewed over and over again as they grow older and possibly have their own children. As a result, the sentencing of the offenders indulging their grubby desires in cyberspace are not reflecting community sentiment, and the victims remain voiceless.

15

The mind of a monster

Imagine finding bags of cocaine stacked up at your mailbox, accompanied by a note from a complete stranger suggesting you might like to try some. Implausible, right? Well, researchers give that example in chronicling the incredulous excuses some offenders offer once they've been apprehended on child sex charges. Their defences make a mockery of the charges they face. Some will tell a judge that they stumbled across a child pornography site. Or it just popped up on-screen without any warning. Or it was a noble episode of investigative vigilantism. Or the product of an underlying mood disorder. Experts say abusers can be remarkably different in occupation, educational standards, socioeconomic status, age and almost every other marker. 'The one characteristic they have in common is denial,' says Dr Joe Sullivan.

Sullivan, from Ireland, knows this cohort. An international forensic psychologist, for the past two decades he has worked with police and prison officers, social workers and schools to try and explain the motivations and behaviours of child sex offenders. Their denial is understandable, he says, because they have 'absolutely no vested interest in revealing the full extent or the nature of their behaviour'. That would mean they'd find themselves in more trouble. 'So they have a very distinct vested interest in minimising, rationalising or flat-out denying that they are responsible for what they've been accused of,' he says. 'That one characteristic is common to every one of these guys.'

The defences, excuses and minimisation techniques employed by the predators described in this book illustrate Sullivan's point. 'I thought it was a passing thing that would go away,' said Shannon McCoole, who was arrested in South Australia during Operation Rhodes.[1] 'I'm not a predator,' claimed Peter Truong, despite being jailed for being one. He continued: 'I'm not a deviant person by nature. I'm locked up with a lot of predators here who have gone out and raped and done a lot of very bad things to child[ren], and that's not me.'[2]

From 2008 to 2021, Dr Michael Bourke served as the chief psychologist for the United States Marshals Service. Now a private clinical and forensic psychologist, he has provided treatment to sex offenders in prison for almost a decade. 'I treated over 1000 sex offenders and worked with them and I didn't cure one person,' he says. That confession easily gives rise to questions about the use of taxpayers' money. Bourke knows that, and he has an answer ready: 'That's not our model. The model that we use is not a curative model. No-one knows how to cure paedophilia. If anyone did, I would strongly urge them to put us all out of business. I'm a smart guy, I'll find something else to do.'

Throughout this research, every time I questioned the motivations, characteristics and pathways of an offender, I was referred in two directions: to Dr Michael Bourke in the United States, and to Dr Joe Sullivan in Ireland. Combined, the pair have almost eighty years of experience working with child sex offenders across private practice, in prisons and in the court system. They've studied thousands of them, close up and from afar – treated them, interviewed them, analysed them. The obvious first question to pose is just how many child sex offenders are there? The answer: it's impossible to determine. That's because, as discussed in the previous chapter, to be convicted as a child sex offender in court means clearing a dozen or so hurdles. But estimates from these experts, and many others, are that up to 3 per cent of people in the community have an unhealthy sexual interest in children. 'Around the world,' Bourke says, 'that would be tens of millions of people ...' Of course, not all of them act on that interest, but still, the number is borne out by the investigations. One online child sex abuse group had more than one million users when it was closed down by Taskforce Argos. And a recent report by the WeProtect Global Alliance says that three million accounts were found to be registered across the ten most harmful child sexual abuse sites on the dark web.[3]

So what does an abuser look like? And what's the motivation for this heinous crime? Even there, the differences between those convicted can stand out, but Sullivan says broad patterns emerge. Some are driven by a sexual fascination, others by a ruthless desire for power and control, where they derive pleasure from being able to manipulate children. Others still – the more sadistic ones –

want to see children distressed and in pain. 'But they're not all the same by any stretch of the imagination,' he says. Bourke conceptualises offenders into four categories: those attracted to children, those for whom hedonism trumps moral behaviour, those who have antisocial traits like psychopathy, and those with other deviant predilections.

However, none of those traits may stand out if a paedophile knocks on your door. That's because they can be judges and jokesters, police and prostitutes, teachers and tradesmen, business owners, entrepreneurs and academics. 'These men and women are in our society. They're literally the person next door. In some cases they're school teachers, they're clergy, they are youth organisation leaders, they're anyone who has access to children,' says Bourke. 'There is no particular ethnic background, no particular job or socioeconomic status ... that is necessarily diagnostic of someone who would be interested [in] or who would act out against the child in a sexually abusive way.' These predators can hold a position of trust where they are able to win over a community or organisation that has children in its care. That provides a key ingredient for abuse: access. Bourke explains: 'One of the best ways to earn that trust is with positional authority – to be the priest or the rabbi or the pastor, or to be the head coach, or to be the principal of the school or someone else that has respect in the community.'

Seeking out these positions also helps establish 'moral compensation', a term used by Bourke to explain how many paedophiles are able to compartmentalise their criminal behaviour. 'They know in one of the compartments of their life that they're doing evil things,' he says. They are hurting children, indulging in antisocial behaviour which runs counter to the expectations of their community or faith. 'Yet they're able to overcome all those inhibiting factors by justifying and rationalising and intellectualising and denying all these things [which] we call cognitive distortions,' says Bourke. They are able to 'build a bridge' and find ways to validate their abhorrent behaviour. They can insulate the shame and self-loathing prompted by their behaviour by appearing to be morally upstanding, a pillar of the community. 'That allows them to sort of balance the seesaw and say, "Well, I'm not a horrible person. I just have this one little section of my life ... everybody is imperfect. And look at how many houses I've built for the homeless and how much good I've done in the soup kitchens."' They try to recalibrate their moral compass. Bourke adds that, as a clinician, he found some of their charitable works were not done for public recognition either: 'They wanted to do something good because they knew that they were doing something bad.'

That analysis goes to why in some operations, like Auxin, so many community leaders were led into police vans: childcare centre owners, police, businessmen, educators. Rouse says more than 40 per cent of those apprehended in some police stings were married with children. 'They have the same jobs as the rest of us,' he says. But Bob Atkinson, who was a commissioner on an inquiry into institutionalised child sex offending, says they can also simply be opportunistic 'grubs'. He nominates two broad types of predators: the opportunist who might, say, hook up with a single mother to access a child, and those with the skills to groom people – not only children, but families, organisations and communities. 'And they're calculating, they're predatory and they're totally committed,' says Atkinson. The majority of contact child offenders are also known to their victims. Atkinson, who had a 44-year career with Queensland Police, eventually becoming its leader and later taking on the royal commissioner role, says he's seen every type of criminal activity, from 'drunken stupidity to organised crime'. But, he says, 'the people who practise in this trade of online child abuse, they are in a purely evil basket. The most fundamental thing for all of us is food, shelter, and water and safety, and particularly with kids. It doesn't matter what country it is, that's the most fundamental basic thing – that you protect children. And this is the opposite of that.'

Arnold Bell, who held senior roles in America's FBI for many years, agrees. He's dealt with kidnappers and murderers, drug lords and violent armed robbers. But child sex offenders? 'They're the worst of the worst of humankind,' he says. 'Every person I've ever interviewed in this crime type claimed to be a victim when they were [a] kid. It's like, "You'll be sympathetic to me because it happened to me."' Of course, many of them might have been abused themselves, but Bell's point is that offenders, almost always, are utterly untrustworthy. Many of them play the victim card and deny the seriousness of their offences. 'Living with a paedophilic disorder is a life of perpetual anxiety, crippling fear and debilitating depression,' Benjamin Faulkner told a court.[4] 'I didn't want to be this way. I had quite a lot of self-loathing. I still do,' said Shannon McCoole, the Australian head of a dark web club.[5]

Dr Michael Bourke says: 'I've worked in prisons since I was nineteen years old. I've worked in ten different jails and prisons in my career. And I wouldn't trust anything that any inmate said.' But, he says, sex offenders are often worse than others, because their crime has been revealed to the world, the facade of being a good, upstanding citizen torn away. 'And they're much less likely to tell the truth about what they've done. Even in treatment, we'd have a hard time getting them to tell the truth.' Paul Griffiths agrees that child sex offenders cannot be believed: 'They will just say what they think is the best thing to say at that moment in time to either divert the attention from themselves or to make you satisfied that they've given you enough information just to get out of whatever position they're in at that time. They'll just tell you whatever it is that you want to hear.' Some might even believe their lies.

Remember that Far North Queensland father and paedophile Mark Newton told a court this: 'Being a father was an honour and a privilege that amounted to the best six years of my life.'[6] It was during those six years that he trafficked his child for sex to men around the world.

•

Dr Joe Sullivan says the myths about child sex offenders run to a long list, but a couple stand out. For example, he says those with a sexual interest in young children are likely to offend against boys and girls, not just one gender. And while online offenders are almost exclusively men, women are nonetheless amongst them – and their crimes are often worse. Indeed, Dr Michael Bourke says that, in the cases he has worked on over a long career, the most egregious forms of sadism, including extreme forms of torture, were perpetrated by women. Sullivan also says that, in his experience, many of those caught offending online have already committed offences in the 'real' world.

Matt Tyler, Executive Director of Jesuit Social Services' The Men's Project, which oversees Stop It Now! Australia, says the average age at the onset of thoughts about offending against children is around fourteen – quite early. The average age at the first arrest is twenty-four. Sullivan confirms that awareness of an interest in children surfaces at puberty, but he believes most have acted on it by the time they become an adult at eighteen. 'So, when you're talking about a 55-year-old man who's been caught for the first time downloading indecent images, that won't be the whole story,' he says. Of course, the offender will claim it's the first time it's happened, that it occurred without prior planning. 'But when you delve into their stories,' says Sullivan, 'the vast majority of them have been aware of this interest before they even got on the internet.'

My research for this book, while it was focused on online child sex abusers, raised other questions: Are they any different from offline perpetrators? Does one lead to the other? Is one worse than the other?

'The content that we're seeing is making it significantly easier for people to gain access to content that will impact on their thinking on their arousal patterns,' says Sullivan. When he began working in this area, the internet didn't exist, and a huge cache of sex abuse images would be 150 photographs. 'That was being gasped at as being an enormous collection of images,' he says. 'Now, terabytes of images are becoming the norm.' Some people might also have developed their behaviour patterns 'beyond what they would have done' had access to the material on the internet not been possible. So there's no doubt the role of the internet in child sex abuse is mammoth – some offenders believe it offers them anonymity in trading evil, that they won't be found, while others are drawn to increasing their sex abuse behaviour in order to join child abuse clubs on the dark web. But that aspect aside, the motivational pathways for offenders who operate online 'are identical to those that operate offline', says Bourke. 'And in many cases, those are the same people.' Indeed, estimates from different experts all sit at around three-quarters of offenders online also having offended offline. Sullivan, who has interviewed these offenders for almost forty years, says more than 80 per cent of those caught downloading indecent images will admit during the course of therapy to having engaged in 'undetected, contact sexual offending prior to their online activity'.

Dr Michael Salter from UNSW, an expert in child sexual exploitation and gendered violence, agrees that online and offline offenders are similar cohorts. 'They have sexual impulses towards children, otherwise they wouldn't be seeking out sexual material,' he says.

Differences certainly exist between the offences committed online and offline, but more in relation to the process involved and how they are dealt with by courts than anything else. As described earlier, online networks are run according to a company structure, with reporting lines, secure access and regular testing to ensure outsiders don't sneak in. Sometimes in these cases, the key character is the administrator or the technical guru who enables encryption to evade detection. Strip all of that away, however, and, inside, they're the same people as offline perpetrators. But couldn't someone just be looking online? 'You don't fall across this stuff,' says Rouse. 'You have to really, really go looking for it.' Bourke says: 'If the question is, would someone be solely voyeuristic online but not be voyeuristic offline, I don't know any studies that have shown that.'

Recently retired US Department of Homeland Security's Jim Cole explains the crossover between online and offline offences with analogies involving Arabian horses and Corvettes. He says if you love Arabian horses, you might look up photos of other horses, but mainly ones of Arabian horses. 'If you're really [a] hobbyist,' he continues, 'you're at least going to want to have interaction with Arabian horses. They're expensive. So maybe you don't own them, but maybe you do. So there's this progression that happens.' Or, if you are a Corvette enthusiast, you would want to work up to buying a Corvette. 'And you want to drive the Corvette. You want to own a Corvette. It's no different,' says Cole. Someone who is sexually attracted to children and goes online might start collecting imagery, but, says Cole, it's 'not like at some point the pictures are enough [and they say] "I'm going to stop here". It's progressive and that's human nature.'

Lianna McDonald from C3P in Canada says the 80 per cent figure raised by Bourke is unsurprising, and that many offenders are 'leveraging technology to their advantage'. She says: 'You cannot package this as a facilitated technology-only related problem. The villain is everywhere amongst us. We know that from what we do, through the work we carry out.'

The first detailed look at the differences between online voyeurs of child pornography and 'hands-on' abusers was undertaken by Bourke and Andres Hernandez in the mid-2000s. Conducted at the Butner Federal Correctional Complex in North Carolina, the study found that internet offenders were significantly more likely than not to have physically abused a child. It also asserted that abusers were likely to have multiple victims and to have crossed over both age and gender lines. A report stemming from the study said: 'In our work with hundreds of Internet child pornography offenders in treatment, the vast majority of those who denied paraphilic interest, subsequently acknowledged their pre-existing and longstanding sexual interest in minors.'[7]

It should be remembered here that while this study occurred in the 'internet age', it predated the ubiquity of portable devices and wireless technology that has facilitated widespread filming and uploading. Yet it points to a complex crime ecosystem in which online investigations have also led to the apprehension of contact molesters. 'If it had not been for their online criminality, these offenders may not otherwise come to the attention of law enforcement,' says the report.[8]

•

A cure, it seems, is out of the question. Dr Joe Sullivan says, 'You're not talking about something that can be cured, you're talking about something that can be controlled if the person chooses to do that.' Indeed, therapeutic intervention programs are directed at helping offenders to develop skills to learn how to control the urges they will live with for the rest of their lives. While it simplifies the issue, and mutes the seriousness of child sex offences, how we deal with alcoholism offers an example here. Like child sex abuse, there is no cure for it, but a learned skill set can deliver abstinence. Still, the difference between sobriety and cure remains.

Bob Atkinson says the curbing of child sex offences could be supplemented by other approaches – such as electronic monitoring, paedophile registers, and supervision and therapy programs – to reduce the risk to the community. He does understand how difficult it is for the community at large to take in untruthful, repeat child sex offenders. 'I think we are an incredibly forgiving society,' he says. 'So you can put your hand up and say, "Hey look, I've got an alcohol problem," and we'll support you. You can say, "I've got a drug problem," and we'll support you. You can say, "I've got a gambling problem," and we will support you. You can even say, "Look, I've been terrible to my partner, can I do a rehabilitation program?" and we'll probably be supportive. You put your hand up and say, "I think I'm a paedophile," and [that support] is not going to happen.' But it should, says Atkinson. 'And they should be able to do it anonymously and [with] confidentiality and get the support.'

Dr Michael Bourke says feelings around improper sexual behaviour often surface at the same time peers are discovering their own – more normal – sexual preferences. To whom are they attracted? What is their sexual orientation? This tends not to change very much through their life span. The same thing happens with people whose sexual interest is in children. According to experts, from puberty to the first offence being committed, likely between the age of eighteen and the person's mid-twenties, there's a window of opportunity where children who are on that trajectory can be targeted to receive help.

'Hating is not a solution here,' says Jon Rouse. 'We need to bury the hate.' That sentence is understandably surprising. This man, for decades, has had to deal with the worst possible offenders. At one point I ask Rouse: Who is the worst paedophile you've encountered? It's impossible to determine, he responds. How do you compare someone who kills their victim with someone who tortures them for years and allows them to live, with the constant reminder of their torment being shared around the online world for the rest of their lives? How do you compare the uncle or grandfather who obliterates the trust of a child under the guise of a night-time story, with the psychopath who writes down every minor detail of his plan to abduct a schoolgirl, cut her open and sexually abuse individual organs? And he says we need to 'bury the hate'?

But there is no doubt that early intervention is the key to reducing the number of men and women who travel down the path of abusing children. That involves a host of programs that can target young children who exhibit problematic sexual behaviour. It also means there's a need for specialist health services for those who recognise their behaviour and want to address it, before they act on it.

Stop It Now! Australia provides counselling and support to those who seek it. Its impetus came from the Royal Commission into Institutional Responses to Child Sexual Abuse, which showed that we were missing a crucial prevention window – one that, according to Matt Tyler, 'is not being missed in other countries'. Run in other nations, including the United Kingdom and the United States, Stop It Now! is an anonymous, confidential service targeting those who experience concerning sexual thoughts and behaviours. The Australian arm was only set up in late 2022 but it is already being flooded with calls and its website has received thousands of visits, via two channels: police referrals, and pop-up messages delivered by a range of technology companies when someone goes searching for illegal material. Based on the evidence from overseas, it appears possible to make a dent in a market no-one wants to see flourish. So far, the service is only for adults, but Stop It Now! has children calling, too, and hopes to expand its services, under a different practice model, over time.

The point made by Bob Atkinson about the community's attitude towards sex offenders will always make gaining support for a service like this a challenge. That has prompted Stop It Now!, which is funded by philanthropy, to work with victims' groups like Bravehearts to understand the perspective of those who have been hurt, injured and assaulted by paedophiles. The idea that the service was 'helping paedophiles' is difficult for some to accept, but most are strongly supportive because, according to Tyler, it may 'prevent what happened to them happening to someone else'.

Georgia Naldrett, who has a master's degree in forensic psychology and who worked at Stop It Now!'s equivalent UK organisation until 2022, now manages the Australian operation. She says the overseas experience shows the service being used by people of all ages, from sixteen to eighty. 'And what that research suggests,' she says, 'is that individuals who reached out to the helpline felt more able to identify how the behaviour was harmful, felt more able to manage their behaviour, and felt that they had more power to move forward and not commit offences in the future.' The key is to offer help before the offending begins. 'We seem to fixate a lot in the public about warning signs that abuse has occurred, which 100 per cent plays its role. But I think the shift to looking out for warning signs that abuse may occur is even more powerful,' says Naldrett.

That's a widely shared view. Sullivan says: 'I've yet to meet someone who's done it once and decided that that was terrible, and then never do it again. I think once they've got over that barrier of guilt and fear and shame, then it's very difficult to return from that. I think there are some who become frightened by what they've done, who maybe will moderate their behaviour, whereas there are others who speed up and just become more and more prolific.' There's no way of estimating the average number of victims per perpetrator. 'But it'll certainly be more than the one or two that they've been caught for,' says Sullivan. 'In some cases, it is hundreds, in some cases it's thousands, depending on the type of offending that they engage in.' And none of those individuals are 'low risk', a term Sullivan says has 'slipped' into our parlance, to the point where it is now being used in courts to denote someone perceived to have less likelihood of reoffending. 'In actual fact, that term doesn't talk directly to reoffending,' says Sullivan. 'It talks about re-conviction, which is quite a different beast altogether.'

Bourke makes a similar point, though in a different way. He says some people see a dichotomy where there are contact abusers and then others 'who just looked at a computer'. He continues: 'If you have a victim-centred approach and talk to victims of online child sexual abuse material, they would say that they're victimised every time someone views their image. They see and experience the horrors of being victimised on a daily basis, and that abuse has been memorialised for eternity.' This is borne out by research – for example, according to NCMEC, more than 985 graphic social abuse images and videos of eleven boys aged six to ten were found in caches seized from more than 16 500 offenders.[9] Bourke says the manipulation of a child who is incapable of giving consent, or the production of a child abuse image that is then sent out into the online universe, can – and has – lead to suicide, or lifelong mental health challenges. 'I would say that's a dangerous person,' he says.

Part 6

Hope, danger and a plea

16

Balancing hell with hope

Hope is the currency that sustains the crop of crime fighters introduced in this book – a hope partly rooted in experience, in the knowledge that their work might allow another small child to be brought to safety. That's their North Star. An arrest rarely rates on their motivation meter, nor does a guilty plea, nor a sentence that sends a paedophile to jail for decades. These are important, of course, but it is that rescue, when a child is made safe and gifted the opportunity of a brand-spanking-new future, that drives them. Every investigator has one of those stories, which they keep close to their heart. Because they know the next case file is sitting on their desk, begging to be opened. Another child needs to be rescued. And then another. And another.

Former Queensland police commissioner Bob Atkinson believes investigators of child sex crimes all share a trait that fuels this hope: being able to compartmentalise the work. It's not easy, often done with a heavy heart, but these people have the capacity to close one door while opening another.

Atkinson, himself a global leader in policing, says he's seen the same trait outside the police service, in individuals who are strong leaders: 'They have the ability to go from one thing to another, and few of them dwell on things.'

Dozens of interviews with investigators prove that point. Warren Bulmer, for example, has spent more than two decades, across dozens of countries, trying to identify the victims of online child sex offenders. The images he's seen show unthinkable human depravity, the innocence of an infant or child being damaged in the most awful ways. Most of us might see hatred in those images, but Bulmer says he sees hope – and so he'll spend days, weeks or even months trying to extract vital clues from the photograph or video in front of him.

Take this example, which led to a 36-year prison term for a US-based offender. Bulmer was working on a global case where children were being sexually assaulted, and the images of those assaults were then shared electronically within a mammoth online child abuse ring. He noticed a can in one of the images. It was almost unnoticeable, indistinguishable, but with image-enhancing software he was able to rebuild and read the label. It was a particular brand of beer, and one of the adults in the awful image had been drinking it. Further investigation revealed the brand was produced by a brewery in Pennsylvania and was only available in twelve states in one corner of America. Then came the information – followed by a surge of hope – that the beverage had only been distributed to six of those states. That big hint was sent off to local investigators. Meanwhile, further inquiries tied a distinctive pair of child's glasses to the room in which assaults had occurred, glasses that were only sold at a limited number of ophthalmologists in a particular geographic area. Bingo. The pieces of the jigsaw came together when the ophthalmologist who'd prescribed the glasses recognised one of the victims. The perpetrator was sent to jail, but crucially, his victims were rescued. Hope, delivered in a beer can.

Bulmer says he doesn't draw more pride from one investigation over another. He doesn't evaluate his contributions in that way. But he says he will never forget the first case, where he received a phone call alerting him to his role in a rescue. 'We've now rescued the kids and arrested the offender and you're directly responsible for that.' They were the words he heard, and he remembers every one of them. Bulmer is a big man, covered in ink – in a tussle in a dark alley you'd want him on your side. He's also a serious man, and this is the only time during our interview that there's a real hint of a smile, a tiny one. I ask him how he felt getting that call, and driving home from work that night. He doesn't much care for the question, but he still gives an answer, one that mirrors those of his colleagues: 'There was some emotion, obviously. But then there was an immediate, "Alright, give me the next case. Let's go."'

Hope builds hope. Indeed, as I conducted my research, an impression grew that investigators often pitch their expectations low so as to allow hope to take off.

Bulmer says that once he's undertaken his victim identification work and passed it on to another investigative team, he considers his contribution to be complete. 'I hope it works out,' he says – that word again. Usually, investigators don't hear about what happens next. 'But then,' says Bulmer, 'when somebody comes back and says, "Hey, because of you, we've done X," you go "Wow". You don't really know how to react at first.'

This hope clings to those who are rescued. Bulmer says that he and his peers rarely invest time in what happens to offenders as they wind their way through a judicial system. 'But I know that from that day forward, the kids are no longer being abused,' he says. From that point forward, he assumes life will work out, that most victims are so young that strong therapy will help them chart a full adulthood – a positivity that's borne out by the testimony of counsellors who work in this area. But Bulmer also agrees with Bob Atkinson about the skill of being able to compartmentalise operations and images, successes and failures. 'You don't want to be a robot,' he says, but you have to be able to 'check your emotions'. He adds: 'Your normal human reaction is to want to know what's happening [to the victim survivor]. But for us, you can't – because it will drive you insane.' Hope, the counterbalance.

Sometimes, although not often, investigators will hear second-hand how a child who was rescued is faring years later. Sad stories are plentiful, but so are the happy ones: school graduations, university degrees, having children of their own who they cherish and treasure in a way only someone who has shared their childhood could possibly understand. Almost all investigators are content with that. They know they can't afford to dwell on what's unfolded since that individual was saved from a single night of torment or years of torture. Perhaps this is driven by hope, too, an optimism that is the key to moving on to the next case in search of new clues.

Anders Persson, the well-respected retired European and Interpol crime fighter, says that many of his colleagues and friends asked him the same question: 'How can I work with such cases?' His response? 'I always told them that we can make a difference for the victim.' Persson draws a parallel with his police peers who work in homicide. 'In a murder investigation,' he says, 'he can just find the perpetrator. The victim is already lost. He or she is dead.' But in the work Persson spent much of his life doing, every day presents the possibility of identifying and saving another victim. 'It was very rewarding work because every successful case gave a new life to that victim,' he says.

Furthermore, Persson objects to my suggestion that investigations 'close'. They don't, especially online, he says. There can be more clues, more hope. Some investigations might long lie idle in a database, but sooner or later the tormentor will make a mistake, or a new image will pop up that points to them. 'Sooner or later the missing piece of the puzzle will turn up,' says Persson.

For Bruce and Denise Morcombe, who were thrown into the national spotlight when their son Daniel was abducted and murdered in 2003, every day delivers a reminder of what their son might have been doing now. But they've used their grief to drive hope, ploughing their energy into the Daniel Morcombe Foundation, which provides safety education for children. Along the way, they've seen the almighty impact of those officers attached to Taskforce Argos and other units who have shared their hell with them. 'We still see it today,' says Bruce, two decades after his son's murder, referring to the undercover officers who had to live a lie in order to find the truth about Daniel.

'We met them and some of them were clearly upset and emotional with the job they had to perform,' he says. 'Apart from the badge, they are ordinary human beings.' Those largely unseen police workers, who had to write the scripts for how each day might unfold, were part of the team. Their brief was required under law so that the covert operation was beyond reproach, but the toll was evident in those who lived it, says Bruce Morcombe. The hope shared by all is that fewer children and officers have to endure this hell.

Jon Rouse says every win helps: 'You wouldn't get out of bed and go to work every day if you didn't have wins. We've had big wins in law enforcement globally. We are working better together now than we ever have. We are communicating in real time across multiple agencies around the world on covert undercover work and victim identification work. That didn't exist when I started.' Cold case reviews flagged for 2023 and beyond, resurrecting for new scrutiny those cases that were buried because of a lack of leads or time or resources, offer possibilities too. 'I never give up hope,' says Rouse. 'We are always looking for that one piece of the jigsaw that is missing.'

Victim identification expert Paul Griffiths is matter-of-fact about this topic. 'We do what we do because it's the right thing to do,' he says. 'I've got jobs where we've identified 100 kids and it might have only taken a couple of hours work. And equally we could spend six months and not identify a child.' Investigators win almost every day, he says. Several times a week, an email will pop up thanking Taskforce Argos for the tip that solved a case somewhere in the world. But it would be impossible to identify all the children being harmed. Hope, tempered by reality. 'I think some of the wins we do have is that we make headway in countries that we previously wouldn't have, or we encourage people to look at the problem in a different way, encourage them to divert resources to an issue that they probably hadn't previously considered,' says Griffiths. 'All of those are wins. There's no KPI sheet to record those on, but we know that all of them are having an effect.'

Everyone in this field deals with the job in a different way. Brenden Power, the Australian undercover operative sent to work with the FBI, says he refused to allow the images to affect him. 'I desensitised myself fairly early on,' he says. It took being regularly exposed to online depravity first up, but he says he didn't let himself dwell on what he saw; rather, he focused solely on the technology and delivery mechanisms behind it. 'There was nothing I could do about it,' he says of the terabytes of photos and footage he looked at as part of his daily undercover job. That abuse had already taken place. Power's energy was better directed at helping to reduce the number of kids being subjected to harm. Wins made up for it, too, when the perpetrators were finally called to account in real life.

Power says his most satisfying day saw the arrest of a US predator who had been employed as a technology expert in Florida. The man was using both his home computer and the company computer as a VIP and senior member of a global child sex group. Online, he would engage with Power, believing they shared a common, grubby interest in young children. Power was there when police smashed down the door of the offender's home and dragged him outside in his underpants. 'He didn't realise what was going on until they then introduced me,' says Power. The man really had thought Power was his online buddy, a like-minded paedophile with his secret hidden inside the dark web. Now, officers were telling him Power was a police agent from Australia who had patiently been collecting the evidence that would be used in his arrest.

Power tells the story with an enormous smile. A baddie taken out, one less paedophile preying on our children. But the satisfaction is balanced out by the little ones he couldn't find while working undercover. 'There was one, a girl on a boat with a couple of gentlemen, and they tracked it all the way down [the US coast] to a gated community ...' The story ends there. Thousands of other children are in the same heartbreaking position.

What about balance, I ask? How do you find balance sitting at a computer screen in another country, living the life of an undercover agent? Power left Australia's shores for his secondment to the FBI as a single man, having never previously been outside his country of birth. 'The FBI flew me to Sydney to talk me through the visa process to get me a passport to get out of the country,' he says. 'They basically put me on a plane, and as soon as I got there [the US], they took me to a conference in Dallas, Texas.' Sitting next to him at that conference was an FBI intelligence analyst who introduced herself as Alicia. She and Power married a couple of years later. Balance, it seems, can appear when it's least expected.

Amanda Frame is an ex-police officer who became a psychologist while in the service. She worked as a police detective in the child abuse area, and later was involved in assessing and monitoring the psychological wellbeing of officers and staff members working in high-stress areas, including that patrolled by Taskforce Argos. Frame left the service ten years ago to focus on private psychology consultations, which continue to include child abuse survivors and the police who investigate these crimes. She says hope is crucial for officers because it signals a 'future'. 'If they're holding hope, there's something positive for them to hang on to.' She says police, generally, like to control situations, and in the context of child abuse, that's difficult. 'They don't know what the outcomes are going to be,' she says. 'They have little control over what's going to happen. And it makes sense that they resort to hope.'

•

While hope fuels the long days of many child sex investigators, and even holds together other parts of their life, distractions are vital. Seconded to France to work for Interpol, Persson says he and his wife set out to learn about different parts of their new home country, including its contribution to food and wine! Paul Griffiths says he has always been able to 'switch off' when he leaves work, but travelling 40 kilometres to get home, alternately by bicycle and motorbike, helps too. 'It's pretty hard to do either of those things and still be concentrating on work,' he says. Warren Bulmer moved to Australia just before COVID-19 struck and subsequently was not able to see his family for twenty-two months. 'Sport has always been my thing, even growing up,' he says. 'I still play golf. If I was in a little bit better shape, I'd probably do other sports as well. But right now I just golf and I fish. I've been fishing since I could walk.' Perhaps, maybe, there's a hint of a second smile. Bulmer once netted a 227-kilogram marlin in Mexico, and a 60-centimetre flathead off North Stradbroke Island, also known as Minjerribah, on the eastern side of Moreton Bay near Brisbane. A tackle box filled with hope.

Amanda Frame says having interests outside work is vital, and police training encourages this. 'When we were doing the induction process for officers and staff entering into these high-risk areas like child abuse, we would highlight the importance of having hobbies and outside activities to get that balance, especially with the nature of the work that they were doing,' she says, adding that exposure to trauma, as a police officer, stretches across divisions and units. Frame goes on to say that 'desensitisation' allows officers in high-risk areas to cope better, and 'detachment' from an offender or a case was part of that process: 'Through that repeated exposure to the same situations, they're learning to remove or lessen the emotion of those situations.'

Despite this, officers are often overprotective when it comes to their families. That stood out during my research, with some – even those on the periphery of investigations – having zero tolerance for sleepovers, or refusing to allow their children to take public transport, or use smartphones, or attend parties as a teenager. Frame says it was something she focused on when dealing with police officer parents, to ensure their work life didn't stymie the independence or growth of their children. Frame's husband remains a police officer, and she says they are mindful of 'checking in with ourselves' in the same way with their own children.

The role of family, for those who have that support, is invaluable. Earlier I raised the difficulties confronted by undercover agents in not being able to share their daily work life with parents or partners or children. 'It is such an area of protection for some of these police,' Frame says. Many, though, suffer without it, unable to share the nature of their work because of its sordid nature, or because it might endanger their family. Amongst police officers, the role of family often extends beyond the home unit to their 'work family'. Rouse says three former members of the Taskforce Argos team will be lifelong reminders of that. Detective senior constable Karl Scholz was on assignment, interviewing a victim, when he developed a dental abscess and became ill, dying in hospital in 2002. Detective sergeant Stewart Kerlin was killed in a car crash while investigating a case four years later. And detective senior constable Paul Meese died two years later after developing a brain tumour.

Rouse himself divorced in 2014 and then remarried in 2019. He and his wife Cilla understand each other's jobs, and the challenges behind them. Rouse admits he draws on support from her and his adult daughter. But that police family remains bedrock for all officers.

Once upon a time, even when Rouse was first transferred to the child abuse unit, the value of psychological support was underestimated. But it's now recognised as crucial in all of our jobs. As a community, we've come to understand the importance of mental health and an effective work–life balance. Rouse says that across law enforcement, there are now systems and processes in place to ensure staff are supported. It's embedded through questionnaires, one-on-one meetings with counsellors, anonymous sessions on request, and regular team meetings and newsletters. 'Generally, police officers aren't good at looking after themselves,' says Rouse. 'We build a crust, build a crust, build a crust.' He says the efforts made in this area ensure staff are well trained, monitored and buttressed.

Dr Michael Bourke, who works with serious child sex offenders, says he couldn't work with child survivors. 'That work broke my heart. When I tried to work with the victims, I was left shaken after every session and it just hurt my soul,' he says. But returning to the subject of hope, Bourke says he sees it in his work with paedophiles. It's everywhere in his field. 'Even though they were telling me dark things, I felt like if I could help get them off the street or help them manage these urges then, sort of directly or indirectly, I would be preventing some future child from ever going through this trauma,' he says. He may never know who he has shielded, he says, but it makes him feel more like a protector. 'I felt called to it. And then I just kept working with the population and learning more about them. And I really feel it's noble work and good work.'

But what about the depravity, I ask, the awfulness of it: Has there been a day where he's wanted to give it up? His answer is immediate: 'No. I don't feel any resignation. I feel a profound inspiration from the work. I think that every day that we're out there, we're making a difference, that there are children who will not be harmed because of the work that we do today. They will not be harmed tomorrow – thousands and thousands of children. I understand an aspect of humanity, a darker part of humanity, than a lot of people see. I've been exposed to it. But the more I'm present to evil, the more I'm aware of good.'

•

Tim Mason plays bass in popular Brisbane-based corporate-gig outfit Hot Sauce with Jon Rouse. They've been friends since their final years of school. Back then, Mason managed a music shop and Rouse poured his income into new band equipment. They've been sharing the stage in two bands ever since. Hot Sauce, in which Rouse plays the keyboard, was created in 1996. Rouse also plays the keytar (a lightweight synthesiser supported by a neck strap) in The Electric 80s Show, a popular band with regular national gigs. Driven by a love of eighties music, it was born in 2010 and, from The Eurythmics to Cyndi Lauper to Van Halen, it plays all the big songs from 1980–89. 'It's the saviour of my sanity,' says Rouse. 'It's just the polar opposite of what I do at work. I guess some people paint. Some people run marathons. I can't imagine a world where I didn't have music.'

'He's always been intense,' Mason says. 'And he has real discipline.' That talent has extended to 'herding cats', meaning band members, agents and event organisers. From the beginning, he was usually the first one at practice, unless his day job stole his time; meticulous in dealing with gig schedules; and could adopt a voice that meant agents never messed with the band. To this day, Mason says, Rouse is always in complete control – except that one time, during Operation Auxin, the huge online child sex investigation that targeted more than 700 Australians. Mason says, 'It's the only time I had to take over. He had a slight meltdown.' Rouse had forgotten the band's power supply. 'We all knew there were other things going on and we know when he's in a funk. We avoid conversations to trigger anything.'

Mason says Rouse could slot into any band with his musical ability. 'Jon has got this ear and he can just nail the exact sound of the original artist,' he says. Rouse admits the band runs a bit like his work unit: to schedule, with an eye on the target. 'What songs are working? What are the next five songs? They really liked ABBA. We need to move that up the set list to keep them on the dance floor.' That's the counterbalance to his day job, the KPI after work – as Lionel Richie made clear in his 1983 hit 'All Night Long'.

17

From plain sight into
the spotlight

The early twenty-first century has been marked by dangers that seem to have appeared from nowhere but actually displayed warning signs that put them in plain sight. The century started with the fear that computer systems would collapse when 1999 ticked over to 2000. Its first decade was defined by the terror attacks in New York City that underlined the vulnerability of our most sophisticated society to a handful of destructively driven zealots. Then came the rolling technology breakthroughs – digital technology that doubled in speed and capacity every eighteen months, simultaneously becoming cheaper and more portable, making it more accessible to increasingly younger users, and those waiting to take advantage of them.

Children becoming adults as this book was written in 2023 were only toddlers when social media began its march, initially through Myspace and then through that platform's derivatives. The smartphone, even with its relatively primitive camera, became widespread as they were preparing for their prep years of school. And the first tablet, with its seemingly limitless windows to entertainment, games and the rest of the world, magically appeared in the market as they were changing from play clothes to school uniforms, and beginning the inexorable trek to adolescence with all the vulnerabilities that journey brings.

Other dangers have been in plain sight, too. Technological disruption has pulverised entire industries – the media, transport and retail businesses have all been up-ended, and the ways in which we are educated, travel and manage our money have all been transformed. Some of this has been for the better, some for the worse, depending on your age and perspective. And then there's the selfie. From birth, our children have learned that every activity is to be photographed and shared with grandparents, aunts, uncles, friends and a broader social network. And if it's a photograph of themselves, it's of even more value. A picture of the Eiffel Tower is just not the same without ourselves appearing in it, snapped at arm's-length.

This self-indulgence has also been accompanied by the evolution of our thinking on social issues, usually for the better. For example, we are more understanding and active in accepting the fluidity of gender and supporting those who have previously been trapped in lives that made them unhappy. We have been more reflective about the wrongs of the past and their influence on the present. High on this list is the recognition of racial wrongs that need to be addressed. Similarly, redress is needed when it comes to the inequity women continue to face in a society where males for centuries have written and enforced the rules. And the past twenty years has seen a burgeoning awareness of the grievous wrongs committed against children by abusers able to find refuge in institutions designed to protect their prey. A succession of inquiries and royal commissions in Australia, as elsewhere in the world, has brought some of the most powerful organisations to their knees, begging forgiveness for the decades of sanctuary they have given these abusers.

The most senior Catholic figure in Australia's history, Cardinal George Pell, was buried in early 2023 after being cleared of personal accusations of child sexual abuse, but his legacy was nonetheless stained by his association with convicted abusers and the belief that he in fact stood between victims and fair outcomes for the wrongs his church had visited on them. The public inquiries, the court cases and the revelations of victims, in the past few decades alone, have provided alarming evidence of the craftiness of deviants in finding ways to snare victims in their evil web – and potential victims are born in their thousands every day.

Again, all of this has taken place in plain sight. There is no excuse for not being alert to the dangers. The dark rooms of orphanages may be a harder place in which to perpetrate evil, but the technology – the mini screens, the 24/7 connection to the wider world, the portable cameras in every pocket – is there for everyone to use. So how have we missed these signals, and others that have been visible? Or more to the point, why is it that some of those entrusted to detect these signals instead shut their eyes to what was happening on their watch?

In Chapter 13, we looked at the role of a leading Australian bank in facilitating financial transactions directed at online child exploitation. The revelations took the jobs of Westpac's CEO and its chairman, and the bonuses of its senior staff, none of whom had the slightest interest in the material their customers were procuring. But they paid the penalty for ignoring what they'd been warned might be taking place – *in plain sight*.

The bank had twelve identifiable customers who were regularly transacting with offshore producers of abuse videos, and who then received those videos on screens in their living rooms or carried in their pockets. But this only became evident in 2018, *six years after* AUSTRAC had warned all banks to be wary of transactions that were frequent, seemingly low in value, and involved agents in countries that the money-laundering agency knew were likely locales for the production of material that showcased violent abuse. In those six years, according to material AUSTRAC provided to the Federal Court, millions of breaches of regulations took place involving transactions as small as tens of dollars, up to those topping hundreds of dollars, with the Philippines, Thailand and Indonesia – all countries Westpac had earlier been told topped the high-risk list.[1]

The bank's CEO, Brian Hartzer, initially told staff it was not a major issue. He reportedly told them that Australians were just going about their daily lives and 'we don't need to overcook this'.[2] No-one else thought the issue was overcooked, though, including Westpac's major shareholders and the nation's most senior political figures, the prime minister and the treasurer. Hartzer resigned, and chairman Lindsay Maxsted announced he was bringing forward his own retirement.[3]

The result has been a renewed vigilance practised by all financial institutions concerning transactions that might fund the abuse of children. What was in plain sight is now in the spotlight.

The same is true of the checks authorities apply to those charged with caring for children, after the case involving Shannon McCoole, outlined in Chapter 10. The South Australian childcare worker ran a global ring of child abuse called The Love Zone, until he was arrested and convicted, hopefully to spend a lifetime in prison for contact offences and the distribution of online material. It was McCoole's access to children through his state's child-protection system that prompted justifiable outrage, and a royal commission which unearthed deep flaws. The paedophile was able to exploit a friendship and some false CV claims – he said he was enrolled to study as a teacher but wasn't[4] – to first secure casual after-school care shifts, and to then become both a contracted and staff worker for Families SA, the agency with responsibility for looking after children from broken families.

The subsequent royal commission report chronicles McCoole's progress through the system, his contact with children, and the assaults on them that he videoed for sharing with his global cohort of abusers – some of the victims were as young as eighteen months old. One older child whom he was not accused of abusing referred to him openly as 'Mr Paedophile',[5] and other case workers noticed unusual behaviour regarding children, some of whom sought to avoid him. This included the inappropriate touching of and occasional abusive comments about the children he was being employed to care for. In one instance, a co-worker believed she had interrupted the attempted rape of a girl, who initially complained of a 'sore bottom' but later refused to discuss it – the co-worker did not report or record the incident until McCoole became the focus of a royal commission. On another occasion, he brought a number of movies to a care house where he was engaged, one of which was entitled *Young People Fucking*.[6] This led only to a caution, on the misunderstanding that this was an MA-rated movie rather than an R-rated one, and his employment continued. In hindsight, noted the royal commission, taking that movie to the care home may have been a grooming tactic intended to normalise sexual behaviour with children.

The report outlines dozens of red flags concerning McCoole's behaviour. Some are comments by children themselves, while others are previously unreported incidents, such as photos of children being taken on McCoole's personal mobile phone, when the childcare worker was only supposed to use an institution-supplied camera – more worryingly, the children were photographed in compromised positions. The report also spells out disciplinary concerns about McCoole, partly in relation to his dealings with co-workers, but none led to him being removed from employment with children. In fact, McCoole was promoted during his period of employment. He was then suspended, investigated and cleared of separate accusations, which allowed him to return to work.

Royal commissioner Margaret Nyland, AM, observed that Families SA and those working for it had failed to respond to these red flags at a number of stages:

Information that should have been actioned was not actioned, reports of concerning behaviour were not made or not adequately actioned and the behavioural communications of children in care were ignored. Had the various red flags been tracked and viewed together or investigated in a more cohesive and comprehensive way, McCoole's behaviour would have received greater scrutiny.[7]

She further observed:

This situation developed in circumstances where the risk of abuse within institutional environments had long been part of public consciousness, where a body of understanding had developed about preventative practices and where warnings within the organisation identified ongoing risk ...

At the time he started working with children, McCoole had a clearly developed sexual interest in children and predatory motives towards them. The characteristics of McCoole's offending, and his characteristics as an offender are particularly heinous. However those working in environments which provide services to children require an understanding that McCoole's activities only represent one form of offending. Systems must be capable of protecting against the variety of circumstances in which child sexual offenders offend. Restricting opportunities to offend can be the most effective means of achieving this result.[8]

As discussed in Chapter 15, the link between viewing sexual assaults on children and performing them is strong, with 80 per cent of apprehended online offenders admitting earlier physical experiences with children – sometimes when they were not much more than children themselves. This pattern of behaviour is now in plain sight, as is the material which can enliven such dangerous instincts.

•

It's clear that the vulnerable are the most likely victims of this criminal behaviour. As detailed in Chapter 1, through the cases of Bridget and Tom, the prime target right now is teenagers – with a rising proportion of boys – who are being persuaded to expose and record themselves sexually on camera and are then blackmailed to either pay money or perform more extreme acts for the salacious interests of global networks of users, in the hope the images won't be broadcast. And new technology is only increasing the potential risks. AUSTRAC, in partnership with its Fintel Alliance, the AFP and the ACCCE, has gone on the front foot to counter this crime after the embarrassment of having its more general warnings ignored a decade ago. In a recent 'financial crime guide' on the theme of combating the sexual exploitation of children for financial gain, it spells out some of those risks.[9] As well as generic internet access, they include the use of social media and gaming platforms, where victims can fall prey to false identities. The growth of blockchain technology, through which cryptocurrencies are traded, also offers a means to obscure transactions.

This renewed focus is producing results, as in one case where a Western Australian man was identified using financial intelligence. The man was sending money to a known child sexual exploitation facilitator in the Philippines. According to AUSTRAC:

Analysis of the payments identified they were for the purchase of child sexual exploitation material and that the offender watched online while victims were exploited in the Philippines. Additional payments identified were sent to multiple adult facilitators and victims within the Philippines and telecommunication applications to enable the live online child sexual abuse to occur.[10]

The offender was arrested and charged with fifty-eight offences, including persistent sexual abuse of a child outside Australia, procuring a child to engage in sexual activity outside Australia, and soliciting and possessing child abuse material. He pleaded guilty and was sentenced in May 2022 to more than fourteen years' jail, 'after paying more than $400 000 to sexually abuse children overseas through a home webcam'. AUSTRAC said the man procured children as young as seven 'to engage in sexually explicit acts or be sexually abused on camera which he watched live from his home'.[11]

An emerging trend is the use of child-like sex dolls to meet sexual urges. Australian legislation now makes it illegal to import or manufacture an anatomically correct, life-sized doll made to look like a pubescent or prepubescent child. One perpetrator, from South Australia, has already been sentenced in the wake of a Fintel Alliance mission to identify such purchases. The man pleaded guilty to five charges that included importing a child-like sex doll from China and possessing child exploitation material. His financial transactions gave him away, as did his multiple purchases of children's clothing including school uniforms and underwear.

'A child-like sex doll potentially normalises behaviour and desensitises an offender from the harm that child sex exploitation causes,' the AUSTRAC report warns. The report also encourages financial services businesses to be on the lookout for another growing practice: the purchase of bereavement dolls, initially produced to replicate a deceased child to assist parents with the grieving process, but bought by offenders for sexual purposes. 'Financial service providers should also use enhanced customer due diligence to determine the legitimacy of a purchase.'[12]

We can add to these physical tools the various virtual permutations. Deepfake videos that involve highly realistic computer-generated likenesses have become widespread. They have been used to misrepresent politicians, but crime detection agencies also warn of the ability to substitute a child's image into a sexually compromising situation. While this does not involve the physical abuse of the child, it represents a violation of their image and the opportunity for an enormous number of abusers to view it.

Then there is the development of virtual reality. Jon Rouse says computer games have always been a 'happy hunting ground' for child sex offenders, and now, 'with dedicated communications platforms for gamers, child sex offenders can move the conversation from the gaming environment'. Indeed, in March 2023, Bruce Morcombe revealed an attempt to groom his six-year-old grandson, who was playing Roblox. What will be the impact of augmented reality? Can digital cops police a beat online? What about haptic suits, where the wearer's body can feel impacts: What might that mean in the tawdry world of online child sex?

Rouse says the challenges of the future are in plain sight too. 'We are in a perpetual arms race between industry developing the latest money spinner, kids using it and getting exploited because industry did nothing to safeguard it, parents being clueless to what is happening under their own roof, police trying to mount investigations with inadequate or non-existent legislative frameworks, and an ever increasing and broadening threat matrix,' he says. 'If we fail to continually look over the horizon and commence planning and future proofing [as much as we can] our education, awareness, legislation, policy, investigative law enforcement response, then we are doomed to continue on the mouse wheel that we currently find ourselves on.'

When I first heard all this, it seemed close to the realm of science fiction. But only a handful of years ago, so did the likelihood of children being able to carry around powerful computers that allow them to communicate freely and instantly by video with the whole world. The next changes are closer than a few years away. Many of the dangers are in plain sight. What can you do about them? Read on.

18

A plea to parents

For years I've researched teen girls, their hopes and heartaches as they traverse those tricky years between childhood and adulthood. And with each of the books I've written about them, I've been struck by the ironies that envelop their lives between the ages of eight and eighteen, such as that their friends are often also their tormentors; while non-judgemental of others, they can be brutal in self-judgement; and while they face infinite possibilities, frequently they'll funnel their decisions because of that modern disease of comparison. And those are only some of the ironies that follow them out of bed to school and back home each night. Boasting an awesome inclusivity, they'll quickly cancel the views of those who disagree with them. Gutsy in articulating their own views, they'll often ask a parent – usually Mum – to make a doctor's appointment. While they'll express concern about their economic future, they'll seek purpose over dollars at every opportunity. Hearts brimming with magic, they struggle to know how to use it. And perhaps the biggest irony of all? More connected than ever, many of them are utterly, utterly alone. It's that last one that keeps me awake at night.

Bridget's story, recounted at the beginning of this book, goes to the heart of why I think we have reached a tipping point in parenting. Tom's story, also told in Chapter 1, does too – but to that in a moment. Bridget could be my daughter, or your daughter. She could be anyone's daughter. I imagine she's fun and feisty outside that bedroom door. Mid-teens, definitely. Going on the cases I've been told about, she is probably a good student and a respectful daughter. She might play in the school's top netball team, or play the guitar for fun, or have a part-time job that provides her pocket money. But where is she as the rest of her family responds to a call for dinner? In her bedroom, at a computer, taking orders from a stranger. He could be anywhere – in the same town or the next, another state, or another country. Technology allows that connection, the hard sell by our children about allowing access to social media. But it's how she feels sitting in the bedroom with the door closed, that complete loneliness, that should have us advocating for profound change.

A predator has befriended Bridget by tricking her, making her think the cute avatar that sent her an online note was a peer who knew many of her friends. It was that inclusivity, a trait that runs through our teens, that was probably behind Bridget's decision to accept the friendship request. How many online friends do our children have? How do they check that someone who wants to link up on social media really is who they say they are? Do they know that person as they are in real life? Some young teens have more than 1000 friends on a single social media platform;

older teens boast more. But as popular as they might be, it's unlikely they know every single one of these contacts.

After accepting that initial friendship request, it is perfectly understandable that Bridget – and others like her – would be non-judgemental and even a bit cheeky in chatter. It's the age when teens are working out who they want to be, and perhaps even why they don't want to be like their parents. They wonder about sex if they haven't had it, and perhaps even want to discuss it if they have had an awkward encounter. Maybe it's easier to talk to their new online friend because they might understand in a way that Bridget's close friends don't. And her new friend is happy to share her experiences, too. It's common at that age for girls to worry about the size of their breasts or to wonder what is a 'normal' request from a partner and what is not. Those conversations happen in the schoolground every single day and are part and parcel of teens deciding their own behaviour, value system and individual personalities. So why wouldn't they chat to their new online friend, even send a photograph in response to one they've received? This is between two teens, two peers, two online friends, both trying to find their way in the world.

It's then, when the teen presses 'send', that the cute avatar of Cindy or Lauren or Hazel, who Bridget thought she knew via her friends from netball or soccer or debating or choir, metamorphoses into a monster. The avatar disappears and Bridget is confronted with a nauseating choice. She is told, by this avatar she considered a teen friend, that she can perform a sex act on camera, for her online extorter, or have her breasts, or whatever else she photographed, plastered over the internet for all her friends to see. And her school, where she's hoping to ask a boy in Year 11 to her formal. And her netball community. And her teachers. And people she doesn't even know in countries she might never visit. *And her parents!*

How do we know our own daughter isn't as welcoming as Bridget when someone comes knocking on her online door? Do we think she'd ask more questions? How would she respond if an online peer started asking her about sex or body shape or what she'd like to do with a partner in a year or two? Would she close the computer, or would she willingly confide in her new friend, who is just as happy to share? Most of us don't believe our child will get caught in this position. That's what the school principals who are now dealing with cases of sextortion tell me repeatedly. Parents express shock that this could possibly happen to their clever, sassy, well-behaved child. But it did. Indeed, the ACCCE commissioned research asking parents, carers, educators, health professionals and adult siblings of children whether there was any likelihood of online sexual exploitation happening to their child. About four in five said there wasn't. Only 3 per cent listed online grooming as a concern! And half admitted they did not talk to their children about online safety.[1]

That is a big red flag, especially in light of what I've discovered in the course of researching this book. It is often a teacher or other adult at school who a teen might confide in if she is being sextorted. In some ways, we should celebrate this. It's unlikely in our – their parents' – generation that we would have approached an educator about something so intimate. But it's the reason why teens aren't informing their parents that points to a desperate need for change in the relationships we have with our teens. Why can't they walk out of that bedroom and confide in us? Because they are scared of the consequences. They fear getting in trouble, being grounded, having their phone taken away. They feel enormous shame over having sent that initial image to someone who turned out to be an adult male, and who is now blackmailing them. They're embarrassed. And so, alone, they cop the awful consequences of their teen mistake.

Isn't that on us, as parents? Shouldn't our top priority be for our children to know that no mistake is so big that we can't help them navigate their way out of it? That we might be disappointed or shocked or curious as to why they would send a revealing photo of themselves to another person, when we've repeatedly told them not to, but that we stand ready to help them? That there is a road out of this hell, and it's more important to alert authorities than to acquiesce to creating more intimate images or paying money to stop the images going viral? The contest is absolutely unfair: our children up against either serious online sex predators who are highly practised in their criminal art, or scammers who are probably acting as part of an organised crime network thousands of miles away. How can a fourteen-, fifteen- or seventeen-year-old navigate that without the help of an adult? And if it's not us – their parents – who should it be? Do our children have a list of mentors who they know will always listen to them in a non-judgemental way? If so, that's not a reason for us to feel disappointed, just because our teen has chosen to talk to someone else; rather, it's a gift we can give them.

During my research, one of my daughters moved interstate to university – an emotional time for her and for those of us she left behind, who miss her. But it was a conversation with a friend of mine that provided me – and I hope her, too – with enormous comfort. My friend told her: 'There are some things you might not want to tell your folks, so I'm calling with my number – you can use it any time you like.' One sentence. And that number is now in my daughter's phone. It offers an option she may never use, but she knows she can use it, any day or any night. Do we as parents have someone who would happily take that call? Are we offering to do it for someone else's child? The bottom line is that a child being sextorted needs to be able to confide in an adult. If they are able to do that immediately, before they escalate the number or type of images, there will almost definitely be a better outcome.

My focus here has been on teen girls, who are often a touch younger when approached, and who are much more social on social media. Most have friends they don't know, and many, many have friendship lists that are publicly accessible, which means anyone can call up their account and see who follows them. STOP THIS. That would be the advice of every single expert who appears in these pages. Do not allow your child to have their 'friends' publicly listed, because that means they are accessible to anyone who looks. Set the security measures high, and keep them there. Do any of us – be it at thirteen or eighty-three – really need the world to see who our friends might be? This is one small step, but it will make it much more difficult for those whose predilections are outlined in this book to target our children as prey. Don't forget that with girls, sextorting is almost always around demands that the victim send more intimate content, including videos, which will then be online for years. In almost all such cases, the perpetrator is motivated by sick sexual gratification.

With boys, it's different. Often, when I'm giving talks to parents of girls, I'm asked: What do you worry about most when it comes to boys? I want to scream *THIS*. Writing these next few sentences has taken me longer than writing most of the chapters here, because it is difficult to articulate just how damn dangerous this is for our sons. Of course, this is a generalisation, but as Jon Rouse and all those who spend their days investigating the consequences of online sex crimes will tell you, boys are proving easy game for organised crime syndicates wanting to make a quick buck. That means scammers who send a pretty avatar, wanting to link up. It means those in call centres acting on behalf of crime networks who target their prey with a weapon many teen boys just don't see: an avatar or fake photograph that promises interest in them. Our sons might not want to have long online discussions about the person they may ask to the school formal, or out on a date. They might not want to talk about the sex they've had or the sex they'd like to have. But when an attractive girl comes calling who claims she knows others in their friendship group, their decision to link up online is almost immediate. And if she sends a photo of herself naked, or of her breasts, just to him, in most cases he will acquiesce and send one back. After all, she's sent a photograph of herself, so why wouldn't he return the favour? And when this fake 'friend' asks for a video, many of our sons will oblige, believing this will be a secret between him and the sassy and sexy girl who has taken an interest in *him*.

On all the advice, boys respond faster, are easier hits, and will oblige more quickly. Overwhelmingly, they are also being targeted by another group of predators: those seeking money. These perpetrators will sextort a boy almost immediately they have a compromising photograph – or they might wait for a video, knowing that will bring more embarrassment and shame, and likely a higher price. You read the story of Tom and what happened to him in another country. Rouse says we are now seeing suicides in Australia of boys who are being sexually sextorted. Their age range is higher than the girls being victimised, between fifteen and twenty-four. Some have paid amounts up to $10 000 to stop a video being uploaded by their sextorter. Those who can't pay might be punished in another way, ordered to open a local bank account so that money can be channelled through it and then sent overseas. That allows these criminal networks to escape detection, and it carries the risk of Australia becoming a hub for this crime, which is reaching into homes across Australia. Are our sons confident enough to tell us they are being bribed? Do we – especially fathers – admit mistakes enough ourselves, so that our teens know that making a mistake is just that: making a mistake? What would be our reaction if our fifteen-year-old son told us they'd made a masturbation movie and sent it online to someone they thought they knew but then found out they didn't?

'If you've seen what I've seen, you would not allow your child to take their phone into their bedroom,' says Jon Rouse, who has seen enough of these videos and implores parents to act. 'To see a little girl, twelve or thirteen, with tears streaming down her face at the beginning of a video ... it's sad. She knew what she had to do. And she did.' How does a Year 12 male student focus on his exams when he's being bribed, and feels as though he can't tell anyone?

A warning I mentioned earlier by Susan McLean, the former police officer who now educates schools and children about cyber safety, is worth expanding on. 'Your child is not going to take these naked photos at the kitchen table, I can promise you that,' says McLean. 'Every single one of the images will have come from a bedroom or a bathroom. So they are the two places that digital devices [and] camera[s] should never be, ever ... They [the child] want to listen to music. I don't care. They need a quiet place to do their homework. I don't care. They like to listen to music in the shower by bluetooth speaker ... I see what happens. None of these kids who have been extorted in the past twelve months were anywhere other than a bedroom or bathroom.'

Where is your own child's device? What are the rules around where they are able to use it? Do they have an alarm clock, other than a smartphone, to wake them up each morning? Consider this statistic, reported by ACCCE after widespread research: four out of five children aged four are using the internet, and almost one-third of these children (30 per cent) have access to their own device.[2] At what age is it even appropriate for our children to be given smart devices? Is there anything wrong with our tweens having a 'dumb' device, one that allows calls but no online activity?

Of course, our teenagers' world is largely online, and it's a wonderful world we could not have imagined at their age. It brings new opportunities in education, information and entertainment. It teaches us to cook and run a marathon, connects us with like-minded individuals, and serves as our chief means of communication. Our teenagers need to learn to use it safely, not eschew it. But the question is, at what age? Why are four-year-olds using the internet at home?

Schools need to play a role here, too, taking stock of how devices are being used by pupils. At what age is it sensible to provide a smart tablet to a child in class, and how are they progressively taught to use it? Few primary schools allow children to turn up and start writing with a pen. It's more likely they will start with a pencil and 'graduate' to ink, often after obtaining a 'pen licence'. What is being done in relation to online activity, and how is that monitored at lunchtime or during after-school care?

•

Jim Cole, recently retired from the US Department of Home Security, says he worries about the 'loss of personal connection' he sees with tweens and teens. He wonders whether, as parents, many of us have allowed devices to become our children's 'friend'. 'In the old days,' he says, 'a friend would come over and go play and you'd check in every once in a while.' Now, children are instead playing with their devices and living their lives online. Rather than talking over the back fence or visiting a friend a few doors down, they are all attached to devices. 'We've created a society of kids who have never had to face adversity,' says Cole. 'And then when adversity does strike, it is so overwhelming because they don't have the skills and mechanisms to deal with [it].'

Mike Duffey from the Florida Department of Law Enforcement has this advice for parents: 'Don't let the digital life of your child be their life. Be in their life with them. Be part of it.' Because if you're not, he says, you won't know what strife your child might be in. Duffey says it has become too easy for parents to hand a digital device to a child, as a babysitter.

No doubt, the chief gatekeepers here need to be parents. And that raises the question of how we parent today, and whether the challenges on the horizon demand we rethink that. Most of us know, broadly, the different stages of parenting – those phases we traverse as our children reach the milestones between birth and adulthood. We've seen these change, phenomenally, over time. How and when we feed an infant. How to teach a toddler right from wrong. How we might choose a school and navigate the influence of those outside the family. The trials thrown up by high school, such as friendship issues or bullying concerns, eating disorders or academic anxiety, or any number of other tests of our parenting and our patience. How we judge risk, which often determines the level of independence we encourage in our own children. However, what we thought ten years ago about what we'd be doing with our teens now requires revisiting. We might have charted exactly how to parent across the different milestones, and thought about the importance of being flexible in our approach. But it's the circumstances around us now that need to play the biggest part in how we parent.

As I said at the start of this chapter, we've reached a tipping point, one that underscores the relationships we need to have with our tweens, teens and young adults. We need to understand this clever online world that brings us information on everything from how to change an ink cartridge in a printer to getting the most out of ChatGPT. We need to welcome the enormous opportunities that world offers. But we also need to understand the dangers it poses and provide rules around accessing it that go well beyond the amount of data our children can use. Our children, at eight and twenty-four and every age in between, also need to know that they are able to talk to us, or another adult, anytime. They need to know that, despite any amount of shame or embarrassment, they are able to walk out of their bedroom and tell us about their mistakes. And we need to talk about our mistakes so it's easier for them to articulate their own.

After all my research, including the heartbreaking stories and the awesome work done by our investigators, and listening to their advice, these are my top six tips:

1   Are our children's (and our own) friendship lists publicly accessible? Change this.

2   How many 'friends' do your teens have online? Is it really plausible that they need or even know 1000 peers? Ask them to name them, and encourage them to only connect with people they genuinely know.

3   Where do your teens use their smart device? If it's in the bedroom or bathroom, remove it.

4   Do you understand how the apps they are using work? Parents need to work out the settings, including how to turn off location and chat functions.

5   What is your child's online reach? How many and which platforms, apps and games are they using? How and when are they using them?

6   And this one, which goes to the heart of how an
     online mistake could be dealt with: If your child
     was being bribed by a crime syndicate or an online
     sex predator, would they feel comfortable sitting
     down and telling you? If not, who might they tell?

Dozens of other lessons popped up during my research, but that handful captures the concerns of investigators like Jon Rouse, regulators like Julie Inman Grant, educators like Susan McLean, and international experts like Michelle DeLaune. AFP Assistant Commissioner Hilda Sirec is godmother to seven children, and she wants all of them to have the self-esteem not to be shamed by anyone online. Sonya Ryan, whose daughter, Carly, was murdered by an Australian paedophile, says, 'Create a shield of protection around your child.' And remember that internet use comes with rules, just as we have rules governing the use of a car. Sonya says she's doing what Carly would have wanted her to do. 'It's unfortunate that victims of crime like me have to be the voice on these topics,' she says, 'that things don't change until ... a kid dies or is murdered. I'm really hoping as we move forward that we do less talking and see more action.' Carol Todd, whose daughter, Amanda, took her own life after being sextorted, wants every parent to remember the mistakes they've made. 'Every adult in the world can remember something that they did as a teenager that they didn't tell their parents about, because they were afraid of getting into trouble,' she says. 'But extortion? That's an adult problem. It's not something a kid can solve.'

Sextortion is just one manifestation of the dangers that lie online. The dark web, where serial paedophiles lurk, trading images, paying for rape on demand, and tracking down new children, is more active than it has ever been. The abuse emanating from impoverished countries and driven by economics is more extensive than ever before. This, in turn, provides greater enticements for those with twisted minds. The consequences of an abuse image or video circulating online are devastating. They are almost impossible to remove, and as we've learned, they can be seen millions of times as the victim grows from child to teenager to adult. The advent of new technologies such as deepfakes and augmented reality will take online sex abuse into areas we can't even contemplate yet, and we – parents and policymakers, police, and especially politicians – have a role there.

'Regulation, that is what needs to happen,' says Jon Rouse. 'Industry has proven it is either incapable or just simply unwilling to self-regulate. This is a global humanitarian crisis that is largely overlooked.' At its centre are children like Bridget and Tom. Children are at the heart of the efforts made every day by Rouse and a small team of international crime fighters, who are desperate to rescue them. Children, like our own.

Endnotes

In addition to sources in the endnotes provided here, the author drew from a wide variety of postings, uploads and comments on social media; the notes of detectives who work in this area; and various commissions of inquiry that have studied these issues. The latter include the Child Protection Systems Royal Commission in South Australia, which produced the report *The Life They Deserve*, and the Queensland Organised Crime Commission of Inquiry report. The wealth of research done by the Australian Institute of Criminology, the Australian Institute of Family Studies, the Crime Statistics Agency in Victoria, and the Australian Bureau of Statistics only added to the author's knowledge in this area. So did the documentary *The Children in the Pictures* (2021), directed and written by Simon Nasht and Akhim Dev, and produced by Tony Wright. Resources provided by the National Center for Missing & Exploited Children, the Australian Centre to Counter Child Exploitation, the Carly Ryan Foundation, the Daniel Morcombe Foundation and the Amanda Todd Legacy Society, which are all valuable for parents, were all used in this research. Books like Keith Banks's *Drugs, Guns & Lies* (Allen & Unwin, 2020) offered further insights. In addition, a host of podcasts were used and provide plentiful information to those seeking it – amongst them, *The Children in the Pictures* podcast stands out. The author also referred to the *Hunting Warhead* podcast and the AFP's *Closing the Net* podcast. All of these helped in understanding the issues canvassed.

Chapter 2: From the dark room to the dark web

1   District Court of Queensland, *R v Dobbs* QDC 64, 2015.https://archive.sclqld.org.au/qjudgment/2015/QDC15-064.pdf; Dibben K, '"Australia's Worst Pedophile" Geoffrey Robert Dobbs May Be Paroled', *The Courier Mail*, 27 March 2015. https://www.couriermail.com.au/news/queensland/australias-worst-pedophile-geoffrey-robert-dobbs-may-be-paroled/news-story/4e4ed26d49 df27a141498980eaeb12aa?gclid=EAIaIQobChMIuIOOha-0_ QIV_5JmAh1sDAJoEAMYASAAEgKOS_D_BwE&gclsrc=aw.ds

2   Arthur C, 'Android Dominance of Worldwide Smartphone Sales Goes on, Says Canalys', *The Guardian Australia*, 5 May 2011. https://www.theguardian.com/technology/blog/2011/may/04/android-smartphone-worldwide-dominates

3   Commissioner Michael Byrne QC, *Queensland Organised Crime Commission of Inquiry Report*, October 2015, p. 311. http://www.organisedcrimeinquiry.qld.gov.au/__data/assets/pdf_file/0017/935/QOCCI15287-ORGANISED-CRIME-INQUIRY_Final_Report.pdf

4   Ibid., p. 310.

5   Statista (February 2023), quoted in Le M, 'An Outlook Towards Digital Banking Trends 2023', *VNEXT Global*, 23 February 2023. https://vnextglobal.com/category/blog/digital-banking-trends-2023

Chapter 3: The wild wild web

1   Rowse J, Mullane S, Passed R and Tully J, 'Technology-Facilitated Sexual Assault in Children and Adolescents: Is There a Case for Concern? Fourteen Years of Experience at a Metropolitan Forensic Paediatric Medical Service', *Journal of Paediatrics and Child Health*, 58(3):409–14, 2022.

Chapter 5: The danger next door

1   Roberts G, 'Alleged Online Child Sex Abuse Network Busted By Federal Police, 9 Arrested and 14 Children Rescued', *ABC News*, 4

November 2020. https://www.abc.net.au/news/2020-06-05/afp-ring-alleged-child-sex-offenders-online-queensland/12325618

2   AAP, 'The Sting that Caught Daniel's Killer', *SBS News*, 13 March 2014. https://www.sbs.com.au/news/article/the-sting-that-caught-daniels-killer/cd6o6se5o

3   *The Age*, 'Raids Expose Huge Child Porn Ring', 30 September 2004. https://www.theage.com.au/national/raids-expose-huge-child-porn-ring-20041001-gdypvk.html

4   Ibid.

5   Ibid.

6   *The Sydney Morning Herald*, 'Nationwide Blitz on Child Porn', 1 October 2004. https://www.smh.com.au/national/nationwide-blitz-on-child-porn-20041001-gdju1g.html

7   *The Age*, 'Raids Expose Huge Child Porn Ring', 30 September 2004, https://www.theage.com.au/national/raids-expose-huge-child-porn-ring-20041001-gdypvk.html

8   US Immigration and Customs Enforcement, 'Leaders of "Regpay" Internet Child Porn and Money Laundering Conspiracy Sentenced to 25 Years in Prison', media release, 9 August 2006. https://www.justice.gov/archive/criminal/ceos/pressreleases/downloads/ICE%20Regpay%20PR_080906.pdf

9   Ibid.

Chapter 6: Partners against crime

1   Commissioner Michael Byrne QC, *Queensland Organised Crime Commission of Inquiry Report*, October 2015, p. 361. http://www.organisedcrimeinquiry.qld.gov.au/__data/assets/pdf_file/0017/935/QOCCI15287-ORGANISED-CRIME-INQUIRY_Final_Report.pdf

2   Federal Bureau of Investigation, 'Major Child Porn Ring Busted', 3 June 2008. https://archives.fbi.gov/archives/news/stories/2008/march/innocent_images030608

3   Commissioner Michael Byrne QC, *Queensland Organised Crime Commission of Inquiry Report*, October 2015, p. 361. http://www.organisedcrimeinquiry.qld.gov.au/__data/assets/pdf_file/0017/935/QOCCI15287-ORGANISED-CRIME-INQUIRY_Final_Report.pdf

Chapter 7: Finding Monica and Marietta

1   US Department of Justice, 'Department of Justice Announces Ongoing Global Enforcement Effort Targeting Child Pornographers', media release, 12 December 2008. https://www.justice.gov/archive/criminal/ceos/pressreleases/downloads/JOINT-HAMMER_12-12-08.pdf
2   Smith S, 'Police Crack Global Child Porn Ring', *ABC News*, 6 March 2008. https://www.abc.net.au/news/2008-03-06/police-crack-global-child-porn-ring/1063712
3   *CBC News*, '9 Canadians Arrested in International Child Porn Probe', 15 January 2008. https://www.cbc.ca/news/canada/ottawa/9-canadians-arrested-in-international-child-porn-probe-1.705826

Chapter 8: Millie's rescue

1   Federal Bureau of Investigation, 'Violent Child Abuser and Child Pornography Producer Sentenced', media release, 5 March 2009. https://archives.fbi.gov/archives/atlanta/press-releases/2009/at030509.htm

Chapter 9: Will's silence

1   From an *ABC News* report in 2010, canvassed here: Gorman G, 'A Journalist's Second Thoughts', *ABC News*, 10 July 2013. https://www.abc.net.au/news/2013-07-10/gorman-second-thoughts/4809582
2   Ibid.
3   US Attorney's Office, Southern District of Indiana, 'Hogsett Announces Sentencing of Australian Man in Prosecution of International Child Exploitation Conspiracy', media release, 9 December 2013. https://www.justice.gov/usao-sdin/pr/hogsett-announces-sentencing-australian-man-prosecution-international-child
4   Marr D, 'Gay Couple Lose Son over Child Sex Fears', *The Sydney Morning Herald*, 9 February 2012. https://www.smh.com.au/national/gay-couple-lose-son-over-child-sex-fears-20120208-1rf1c.html
5   Commissioner Michael Byrne QC, *Queensland Organised Crime Commission of Inquiry Report*, October 2015, p. 302. http://www.organisedcrimeinquiry.qld.gov.au/__data/assets/pdf_file/0017/935/QOCCI15287-ORGANISED-CRIME-INQUIRY_Final_Report.pdf
6   Cribb R, Quinn J and Sher J, 'Child Porn Bust: Anatomy of an International Child Pornography Investigation', *Toronto Star*, 14 November 2013. https://www.thestar.com/news/world/2013/11/14/

child_porn_bust_anatomy_of_an_international_child_pornography_
investigation.html

7 *Daily Mail Australia*, 'Depraved Man and His Partner Bought a
   Russian Boy for $8000 and Began Sexually Abusing Him on Film
   from the Age of ONE', 4 July 2013. https://www.dailymail.co.uk/
   news/article-2355194/U-S-Australian-citizen-sentenced-40-years-
   buying-boy-sole-purpose-exploitation.html

8 Walsh M, 'Australian Pair in LA Convicted for Making Child Porn
   with "Adopted Son" from Russia', *New York Daily News*, 30 June
   2013. https://www.nydailynews.com/news/crime/2-convicted-adopted-
   son-porn-article-1.1385895

9 Ibid.

10 *Daily Mail Australia*, 'Depraved Man and His Partner Bought a
   Russian Boy for $8000 and Began Sexually Abusing Him on Film
   from the Age of ONE', 4 July 2013. https://www.dailymail.co.uk/
   news/article-2355194/U-S-Australian-citizen-sentenced-40-years-
   buying-boy-sole-purpose-exploitation.html

Chapter 10: A homegrown monster

1 Commissioner Michael Byrne QC, *Queensland Organised Crime
   Commission of Inquiry Report*, October 2015, p. 299. http://www.
   organisedcrimeinquiry.qld.gov.au/__data/assets/pdf_file/0017/935/
   QOCCI15287-ORGANISED-CRIME-INQUIRY_Final_Report.pdf

2 Ibid.

3 Setter C, 'The Abuse of Children Is Not Constrained By Borders', *The
   Guardian Australia*, 28 February 2018. https://www.theguardian.com/
   global-development/2018/feb/28/abuse-of-children-not-constrained-
   by-borders/

4 Dev A, *The Children in the Pictures* podcast, 'A Perfect Match' (ep.
   7), 8 December 2022. Please listen to the whole podcast!

5 Ibid., 'The Takeover' (ep. 4).

Chapter 11: Covert cops

1 Commissioner Michael Byrne QC, *Queensland Organised Crime
   Commission of Inquiry Report*, October 2015,
   pp. 206–7. http://www.organisedcrimeinquiry.qld.gov.au/__data/
   assets/pdf_file/0017/935/QOCCI15287-ORGANISED-CRIME-
   INQUIRY_Final_Report.pdf

2   US Department of Justice, 'Four Men Sentenced to Prison for Engaging in a Child Exploitation Enterprise on the Tor Network', media release, 12 August 2019. https://www.justice.gov/opa/pr/four-men-sentenced-prison-engaging-child-exploitation-enterprise-tor-network#:~:text=Four

3   Ibid.

4   Høydal HF, Stangvik EO and Hansen NR, 'Breaking the Dark Net: Why the Police Share Abuse Pics to Save Children', *VG*, 7 October 2017. https://www.vg.no/spesial/2017/undercover-darkweb/?lang=en

Chapter 12: Nowhere to hide

1   Commissioner Michael Byrne QC, *Queensland Organised Crime Commission of Inquiry Report*, October 2015, p. 279. http://www.organisedcrimeinquiry.qld.gov.au/__data/assets/pdf_file/0017/935/QOCCI15287-ORGANISED-CRIME-INQUIRY_Final_Report.pdf

2   Ibid.

3   DeLaune M, 'Protecting Our Children Online', submission by NCMEC to the United States Senate Committee on the Judiciary, 14 February 2023. https://www.missingkids.org/content/dam/missingkids/pdfs/Senate%20Judiciary%20Hearing%20-%20NCMEC%20Written%20Testimony%20(2-14-23)%20(final).pdf

4   From conversation by investigators, captured by author.

Chapter 13: Follow the money

1   Australian Transaction Reports and Analysis Centre, 'AUSTRAC and Westpac Agree to Proposed $1.3bn Penalty', 24 September 2020. https://www.austrac.gov.au/news-and-media/media-release/austrac-and-westpac-agree-penalty

2   Butler B, 'Westpac's CEO Brian Hartzer Resigns over Money-Laundering Scandal', *The Guardian Australia*, 26 November 2019. https://www.theguardian.com/australia-news/2019/nov/26/westpac-chief-executive-brian-hartzer-resigns-over-money-laundering-scandal

3   DeLaune M, 'Protecting Our Children Online', submission by NCMEC to the United States Senate Committee on the Judiciary, 14 February 2023, p. 11. https://www.missingkids.org/content/dam/missingkids/pdfs/Senate%20Judiciary%20Hearing%20-%20NCMEC%20Written%20Testimony%20(2-14-23)%20(final).pdf

4   WeProtect Global Alliance, 'The Issue', 2023. https://www.weprotect.org/issue/

5 Australian Centre to Counter Child Exploitation, 'AFP and AUSTRAC Target Offshore Sextortion Syndicates Preying on Australian Youth', media release, 1 December 2022. https://www.accce.gov.au/news-and-media/media-release/afp-and-austrac-target-offshore-sextortion-syndicates-preying-australian-youth

6 DeLaune M, 'Protecting Our Children Online', submission by NCMEC to the United States Senate Committee on the Judiciary, 14 February 2023, p. 10. https://www.missingkids.org/content/dam/missingkids/pdfs/Senate%20Judiciary%20Hearing%20-%20NCMEC%20Written%20Testimony%20(2-14-23)%20(final).pdf

7 Commissioner Michael Byrne QC, *Queensland Organised Crime Commission of Inquiry Report*, October 2015, p. 15. http://www.organisedcrimeinquiry.qld.gov.au/__data/assets/pdf_file/0017/935/QOCCI15287-ORGANISED-CRIME-INQUIRY_Final_Report.pdf

8 Ibid., p. 315.

9 Ibid.

10 Australian Centre to Counter Child Exploitation, 'Scammers Capitalise on Pandemic as Australians Lose Record $851 Million to Scams', media release, 7 June 2021. https://www.accc.gov.au/media-release/scammers-capitalise-on-pandemic-as-australians-lose-record-851-million-to-scams

Chapter 14: Innocence stolen

1 DeLaune M, 'Protecting Our Children Online', submission by NCMEC to the United States Senate Committee on the Judiciary, 14 February 2023, p. 13. https://www.missingkids.org/content/dam/missingkids/pdfs/Senate%20Judiciary%20Hearing%20-%20NCMEC%20Written%20Testimony%20(2-14-23)%20(final).pdf

Chapter 15: The mind of a monster

1 Hancock J, 'Shannon McCoole: "I Thought It Was a Passing Thing That Would Go away", Paedophile Tells Inquiry', *ABC News*, 26 February 2016. https://www.abc.net.au/news/2016-02-26/paedophile-shannon-mccoole-gives-evidence-at-royal-commission/7203970

2 Meldrum-Hanna C, 'The Boy with the Henna Tattoo', *Four Corners*, ABC TV, 10 March 2014.

3 WeProtect Global Alliance, *Global Threat Assessment 2021*, p. 4. https://www.weprotect.org/global-threat-assessment-21/#report

4   Høydal H, Fairless D and Hunting CO, *Warhead* podcast, 'Fallout' (ep. 6), 18 November 2019.

5   Hancock J, 'Shannon McCoole: "I Thought It Was a Passing Thing That Would Go away", Paedophile Tells Inquiry', *ABC News*, 26 February 2016. https://www.abc.net.au/news/2016-02-26/paedophile-shannon-mccoole-gives-evidence-at-royal-commission/7203970

6   Ralston, N, 'Couple Offered Son to Paedophiles', *The Sydney Morning Herald*, 1 July 2013. https://www.smh.com.au/national/couple-offered-son-to-paedophiles-20130630-2p5eg.html

7   Bourke ML and Hernandez AE, 'The "Butner Study" Redux: A Report of the Incidence of Hands-on Child Victimization by Child Pornography Offenders', *Journal of Family Violence*, 24:183–91, 2009, p. 185.

8   Ibid., p. 189.

9   DeLaune M, 'Protecting Our Children Online', submission by NCMEC to the United States Senate Committee on the Judiciary, 14 February 2023, p. 13. https://www.missingkids.org/content/dam/missingkids/pdfs/Senate%20Judiciary%20Hearing%20-%20NCMEC%20Written%20Testimony%20(2-14-23)%20(final).pdf

Chapter 17: From plain sight into the spotlight

1   Federal Court of Australia, 'Statement of Agreed Facts and Admissions', 24 September 2020. https://www.austrac.gov.au/sites/default/files/2020-09/AUSTRAC%20Westpac%20Statement%20of%20agreed%20facts%20and%20admissions_FILED.pdf

2   News Corp, quoted in Letts S and Doran M, 'Westpac Chief Executive Brian Hartzer Quits amid Pressure over Money Laundering Scandal', *ABC News*, 26 November 2019. https://www.abc.net.au/news/2019-11-26/westpac-ceo-brian-hartzer-quits-money-laundering-scandal/11737864

3   Ibid.

4   Child Protection Systems Royal Commission, *Child Protection Systems Royal Commission Report: Case Studies* (vol. 2), *The Life They Deserve*, Government of South Australia, 2016, p. 81. https://apo.org.au/sites/default/files/resource-files/2016-08/apo-nid66267_97.pdf

5   Ibid., p. 97.

6   Ibid., p. 96.

7 Ibid., p. 120.

8 Ibid., p. 140.

9 Australian Transaction Reports and Analysis Centre, *Combating the Sexual Exploitation of Children for Financial Gain: Financial Crime Guide*, December 2022. https://www.austrac.gov.au/sites/default/files/2022-12/AUSTRAC_2022_FCG_Combating_the_sexual_exploitation_of_children_web_0.pdf

10 Ibid., p. 17.

11 Ibid.

12 Ibid., p. 27.

Chapter 18: A plea to parents

1 Australian Centre to Counter Child Exploitation, *Online Child Sexual Exploitation: Understanding Community Awareness, Perceptions, Attitudes and Preventative Behaviours – Research Report*, February 2020. https://www.accce.gov.au/resources/research-and-statistics/understanding-community-research

2 Ibid.

Seeking help

1800 Respect National Helpline – 1800 737 732
Amanda Todd Legacy Society – https://www.
    amandatoddlegacy.org
Bravehearts – 1800 272 831
Butterfly Foundation – 1800 33 4673
Carly Ryan Foundation – http://www.carlyryanfoundation.
    com
Daniel Morcombe Foundation – 1300 326 435
eSafety Commissioner – https://www.esafety.gov.au
Kids Helpline – 1800 55 1800
Lifeline (24-hour crisis line) – 13 11 14
Men's Referral Service – 1300 766 491
PartnerSPEAK – 1300 590 589
Stop It Now! – 1800 01 1800

Acknowledgements

Too often in life, the noisy cog in the wheel gets all the attention. We see it daily, in the headlines that appear on our smart devices, full of whingers and complainers and those who believe they are always hard done by. But every now and again, we get an enlightening peek into the lives of those who don't seek attention but who have a remarkable ability to make the lives of others better.

Often, those people pop up after they suffer dreadful heartache. Denise and Bruce Morcombe, whose son Daniel was abducted and murdered, leap immediately to mind. I'd hide in a corner, I know. But they've used their own sorrow to help ensure others don't suffer their horror. There are many others, and every one of them – whether they advocate for changes to our laws or our thinking – deserve our acknowledgement and respect. In addition to Denise and Bruce, during this project I met Sonya Ryan and Carol Todd, two mothers who have suffered unimaginable grief after their daughters died at the hands of paedophiles. Carol's daughter, Amanda, took her own life after being sextorted. Sonya's daughter, Carly, was murdered by a paedophile she met online, and believed to be someone else. My heartfelt thanks goes to Denise, Bruce, Sonya and Carol. They just want the rest of us – parents and aunts and uncles and carers – to talk to our children, and reduce the risks that stole their own happiness and the lives of their children.

So many others helped in this task, and all showed one common trait. They eschew the noisy cog syndrome, keen to do their work quietly without fanfare, or awards or accolades. They all have these plastered over their walls, and they've accepted them proudly, but almost reluctantly. And always quietly. They want the headlines to be about their work, and the new lives gifted to those they rescue. Warren Bulmer, who you've met in these pages, and who has not seen his family for almost two years, the pandemic cancelling any reunion after he decided to move to Australia and boost our efforts to track down paedophiles and save those they torment. Paul Griffiths, whose talent is talked about across Europe and America, but who also moved here, to raise his family and lead international investigations. Bob Atkinson, the former police commissioner who has devoted decades of his life to public service. In the preceding pages, you've met so many more of these whip-smart investigators, not all of whom live here. There's Arnold Bell, who worked at the FBI; Jim Cole, who worked at the US Department of Homeland Security; Anders Persson, who worked for Interpol; Daniel Szumilas an officer in Germany who stays in his job because he knows the children are always innocent; Australia's eSafety Commissioner Julie Inman Grant; Michelle DeLaune from NCMEC; Mike Duffey from Florida's Department of Law Enforcement; Guillermo Galarza from ICMEC in the United States and Anna Bowden from ICMEC Australia; Lianna McDonald from Canada's C3P; the AFP's Hilda Seric; Brenden Power, who now works with Queensland

Police's Ethical Standards Command; and Dr Rick Brown from the Australian Institute of Criminology. They all have my gratitude for trusting me, and for providing their time and answers to an indefinite set of questions! The same goes to two world experts in this area, Dr Joe Sullivan in Ireland and Dr Michael Bourke in the United States – thank you for taking my calls. The Australian Association of Psychologists Inc (AAPi) has helped me with every piece of research I've asked about, and the role of the psychologist in this field – and almost every other field we can think of, especially post-COVID – needs to be recognised more. So, too, the roles played by our educators and school leaders, who are battling the challenges posed by the online world each and every day. Why don't we listen to them more?

To those who helped me understand Jon Rouse – his wife, Cilla, who is also a senior investigator in the same area; his band mates like Tim Mason; his former bosses; and others who worked on investigations with him, such as Brian Bone and Dawn Ego – thanks for what you do, and for allowing me to see that. The same goes for Bill Potts, Dr Michael Salter, Susan McLean, Georgia Naldrett and Matt Tyler, Keith Banks and Stacey Kirmos, Sharon Lunn, Natalie Walker, Dr Janine Rowse, Amanda Frame and Judge Sal Vasta. This isn't just a list of names. It's a list of people whose body of work makes a material difference to the lives of so many.

Thanks to the clever team at Hachette headlined by Scott Henderson, Rebecca Allen and Kirstin Corcoran, and to Christabella Designs (for the cover). A special thanks to Paul Smitz for his careful editing. It's always good to work with Emily Lighezzolo. And dealing with Vanessa Radnidge makes the long hard days pass faster. The good humour of my husband, David Fagan, a splendid author, helped, along with the home-cooked meals and 5 a.m. coffees. And to our girls, Maddie and Siena, thanks for allowing me to disappear into the home office for weeks on end.

Finally, Jon Rouse, my thanks is on behalf of so, so many people. Those international crime fighters you've worked with, those officers whose careers you've mapped out, but mostly those children, the thousands of them who owe their safety to you and your peers. Thanks for your patience, your willingness to cooperate in this task, and your ability to always see that none of this is about you. Your aim from day one, you told me, was to give a voice to the victims of these awful crimes. Let's hope this helps them become the noisy cog we all need to hear.